LET LOVE CHANGE YOUR LIFE

LET LOVE CHANGE YOUR LIFE

BECKY & ROGER
TIRABASSI

A
JANET
THOMA
BOOK

THOMAS NELSON PUBLISHERS®
Nashville

A Division of Thomas Nelson, Inc.
www.ThomasNelson.com

Published in Nashville, Tennessee, by Thomas Nelson, Inc.

Published in association with the literary agency of Alive Communications, 1465 Kelly Johnson Blvd., Suite 320, Colorado Springs, CO 80920.

Library of Congress Cataloging-in-Publication Data

Triabassi, Becky, 1954–
    [How to live with them since you can't live without them]
    Let love change your life / Becky and Roger Tirabassi.
       p. cm.
    Includes bibliographical references and index.
    ISBN 0-7852-6509-0 (pbk.)
    1. Man-woman relationships—Religious aspects—Christianity. 2. Interpersonal relations—Religious aspects—Christianity. 3. Marriage—Religious aspects—Christianity. I. Tirabassi, Roger. II. Title.

HQ801.T497 2002
248.8'44—dc21
                                            2001044827
                                              CIP

Printed in the United States of America.

01 02 03 04 05 PHX 5 4 3 2 1

CONTENTS

Acknowledgments   *vii*
Preface   *ix*
Introduction   *xi*

Part 1: The Knowledge Necessary for Successful Relationships

1. The Honest Truth About All Relationships   *3*
2. Every Person Is Unique   *20*

Part 2: The Skills Necessary for Successful Relationships

3. Effective Communication   *39*
4. Anger Control   *63*
5. Forgiveness   *73*
6. Conflict Resolution   *85*
7. Financial Management   *95*
8. Sexual Intimacy   *103*
9. Parenting   *112*

Part 3: The Decisions Necessary for Successful Relationships

10. Stay Connected to God   *139*
11. Stay Connected to Each Other   *148*

Chapter Questions   *164*
Bibliography   *173*
Index of the Knowledge, Skills, and Decisions
     Necessary for Successful Relationships   *175*
About the Authors   *176*

ACKNOWLEDGMENTS

Many people have played an important role in our marriage. We would like to thank . . .

our parents for their love and support,

Jake, our son, for being very patient with his parents-in-process,

Jay and Anne Menefee for their educational support, and

Ron and Alexa Jensen for their mentoring and friendship.

In addition, we would like to thank Thomas Nelson Publishers for their assistance in this project—especially Brian Hampton for his patience and insight in editing the manuscript.

And a special thanks to all of our friends who have encouraged and supported us through their prayers.

PREFACE

This book is written primarily to help you develop, achieve, and maintain successful relationships by giving you practical answers rather than theoretical or philosophical ideas. It is written by two people who are not by nature that easy to get along with and who do not find the whole aspect of relationships that easy to master. Both of us tend to be impatient, easily angered, controlling, and critical.

Let Love Change Your Life is written for people in process, by people in process. We write this book for people who struggle with these tendencies, just as we have struggled. Along with you, Roger and I are in the continual process of growing and maturing; therefore, we are practicing the skills and systems in these pages as much as possible. And we wanted you to know firsthand that they have enriched our relationship with each other and with others!

In addition, Roger uses all of these principles and teaches these skills in his counseling practice. Through the use of these proven methods and practical systems for *putting love into action*, he has seen many couples (and families) better their communication, resolve conflict successfully, and grow more deeply in love with each other. Our prayer is that through these pages, you will be inspired, encouraged, and motivated to let love change your life!

Roger and Becky

P.S. This book is written by both Roger and Becky, but (per Roger's suggestion) to make it easier to read and less confusing as to which one is speaking, I (Becky) will write in the first person.

INTRODUCTION

To write a book on love and relationships that would appeal to *both men and women*, I knew of only one expert I could ask to help me with the topic. My husband of twenty years, Roger Tirabassi, M.A., M.S., D.Min., was my first and only choice. He has been the best lover, provider, mentor, and friend a person could ever have in a spouse! But he is not just my personal example of a loving husband. For many years, he has been an excellent teacher, counselor, and pastor to those wanting to achieve lasting love in their relationships.

He has used his giftedness in counseling, besides all of his degrees, to bring insight, reconciliation, and healing to many an adolescent, premarital couple, family, and troubled marriage. The practical systems, skills, and insights that he has learned, developed, and ultimately employed in his practice have been the basis for this book—and truly, the foundation for our marriage. In the examples and illustrations we use, all names and circumstances have been changed. The struggles detailed are not unique to any one couple but are common to many.

Roger has been doing premarital and marital counseling for more than fifteen years. He has developed systems to help couples find satisfaction and happiness in their relationship and avoid divorce. His focus has been on teaching and coaching them in the three areas that lead to successful relationships: knowledge, skills, and decision making.

The *knowledge* necessary for achieving successful relationships includes understanding each other's motivation, the phases of relationships, family of origin issues, as well as recognizing unique differences.

The most important *skills* necessary for successful relationships are communication, self-control, forgiveness, conflict resolution, financial management, intimacy, and parenting.

And the third area, *decision making*, is essential for short- and long-term stability in relationships. The goal for all couples is to make commitments that they will stick to, regardless of the problems that enter their lives.

I am pleased, but mostly privileged, to have my husband, Roger, as the coauthor of *Let Love Change Your Life*. We have written this book with the desire to reach both those who are struggling and those who are striding in their relationships with passionate hope and practical help for achieving a more effective and successful relationship. We know that you will be challenged, strengthened, and stretched, yet our belief is that if you follow these guidelines in detail, you will overcome the struggles you are presently facing, or you will further enhance the quality of your already loving relationship.

The book has been arranged in a manner that builds principles upon principles. For example, listening skills and anger control are taught before conflict resolution, because to effectively resolve conflicts, we need to use listening skills and control our anger.

To maximize the effectiveness of the ideas presented here, we recommend that you read the book from beginning to end. Throughout the book we suggest several sources on specific issues. Our hope is that the practicality of this book will help you and inspire you to grow in the areas specific to your relationship that need improvement.

You'll also find that Roger and I attempt to be open and honest about our relationship. Our hope is that our vulnerability will not only assist you in understanding each other, but also encourage you to be honest with yourself and others.

PART 1

THE KNOWLEDGE NECESSARY FOR SUCCESSFUL RELATIONSHIPS

■ *Chapter 1* ■

THE HONEST TRUTH ABOUT ALL RELATIONSHIPS

As Roger and I grew up, we both remember our dads making that all-too-familiar statement, "Women! You can't live with them; you can't live without them." We also remember our moms responding to our dads by raising their eyebrows, giving a whimsical look, and retorting, "And *men*! You can't live with them; you can't live without them."

It's one of the few statements about marriage that both men and women agree upon! We acknowledge our need to live with a lifelong mate, but we find that *living with them* can be difficult.

Our belief is that living with them can also be a joy if we have realistic expectations, prepare for our inevitable struggles, and make the necessary adjustments for our differing personalities and needs.

EVERY COUPLE IS BOUND TO STRUGGLE

The desire to *live with them* can be traced all the way back to Genesis 2:18, where God said, "It is not good for the man to be alone" (NIV). As singles, we spent much time and energy looking for a spouse, desiring to fill our need for companionship, closeness, intimacy, and a family. Ironically, those of us who married the person we "just couldn't live without" discovered that our differing personalities and needs, our unique idiosyncrasies, not to mention our personal pasts, made *living with them* a challenge!

How can we live with them since we can't live without them? Can it be done? Is it possible? Yes. We believe that you can have a successful marriage by making a commitment to understand each other, develop relationship skills, and make wise decisions.

The first thing to acknowledge about marriage is that every couple is bound to struggle! At a conference, we heard Jay Kesler, president of Taylor University, say, "It is not the blowouts that will destroy your marriage, but the slow leaks." We, too, have found that the day-to-day irritations and frustrations can tear apart the foundation of a loving relationship.

A Perfect Example

The following story describes an actual situation that occurred in our home one morning while we were writing this book. In a span of less than ten minutes, we dealt with many of the issues that this book covers: communicating effectively, playing by preestablished rules, maintaining self-control, understanding how differing needs and personalities interact, asking for and granting forgiveness, and focusing on the positive.

As my assistant was taking her lunch break in our kitchen, unknowingly, Roger and I gave her a live demonstration of many of our relationship principles in action.

I was headed outside to the chaise lounge to have my quiet time, and I saw the garden hose sitting out on the back deck. In a split second I thought, *This hose is just waiting for me to step on it or trip over it*. But I was so focused on getting Roger off the deck so I could get started on my quiet time that I didn't take the time to move it. I rationalized that since he had taken it out, it was his responsibility to put it away.

As I turned to go back into the house to pick up my Bible and get a towel to cover the chaise, I proceeded to trip over that hose, stub my big toe, and holler with pain! As I hopped up and down, I immediately glared at Roger, giving him full "credit" for my current pain. I said, "I just knew this would happen when I saw that you hadn't put the hose away." He smartly responded, "You saw it, thought about it, stepped on it, then you blamed me! What's wrong with this picture?"

Rather than deal any longer with that scenario, I went out to the laundry room to get a towel as my assistant tried not to laugh at me behind her napkin. There I found a dryer full of half-done, damp laundry and another pile of clothes lying on the floor. Still upset and aching from stepping on the hose nozzle, I picked up a clean towel, marched back into the kitchen, and barked, "Roger, if you are going to start the laundry, please finish it. Gosh, I go on a trip for three days, leaving everything in its place, and I come back to hoses and clothes just lying all over the place! Let's start a new rule: Don't start any laundry unless you can finish it!"

Roger had another smart reply, which he directed toward my assistant rather than to me. "Becky's always coming up with a new rule. Three weeks ago she went away, and I found a load of laundry in the dryer that was still damp and very wrinkled." He proceeded to tell the rest of his story with dramatic Italian gestures. "I had to put heat on the clothes for another few minutes, just to get all the wrinkles out. Then I had to bring them into the living room, flatten, and fold them all, piece by piece." He used grand smoothing and folding gestures to show how very difficult it was, but my assistant does enough of her own laundry to feel little sympathy for this singular instance of Roger's domesticity. He continued, "Then I had to put all of our clothes away and go back to finish the load I was starting—simply because Becky didn't finish the laundry before she went away! *But,* now that the clothes are in her way, we have a new rule!" (Roger was squawking about a new rule like the Mad Hatter at his tea party yelling for clean cups!)

This exchange led to a hearty discussion about rules, particularly since we had just written that section of the book. I jokingly suggested that we could make the (laundry and hose) "finish what you start rule" our Rule #14! But my assistant, Jennifer, informed me that we *already* had a Rule #14. Roger had expanded on the rule section in my absence. By that time, we were all laughing hysterically over the ridiculousness of the situation.

Just as things calmed down, we went outside to have our quiet times when Roger noticed Kezi, our big black Labrador retriever, sprawled largely on the lawn. (In fact, just that morning the little neighbor girl screamed aloud, "Look, Mommy, Kezi got fat since I last saw her!") Roger made a comment, "You're just a big stupid dog, Kezi." Even though he said it with a smile in his voice, I jumped on that! I said, "Roger, you broke a rule! You aren't allowed to say, 'Stupid'!"

Roger replied, "You broke a rule too. You aren't allowed to say, 'You broke a rule,' remember? Besides, have you forgotten? I didn't ask for Kezi. When I agreed to let you get Kezi in the first place, you promised that I wouldn't have to walk her, feed her, or pick up after her! But now I do all of those things, all of the time!"

Well, that was an exaggeration. Roger does help with Kezi when I can't do it (and he does love her, no matter what he says).

My assistant quietly piped in from the kitchen, "Roger, remember what you said to Becky before, 'What's wrong with this picture?' Did you really believe that you could get a dog and never have to walk her, feed her, or pick up after her?" Her comment didn't need an answer, and once again, we were all laughing!

By the way, twenty-four hours later the laundry was folded, but on the couch, waiting to be put away, and the hose was still lying in the same place on the deck, and Roger had to take Kezi for a walk that morning.

We chose this illustration because it's an example of a common situation in most homes. Our goal has been to recognize the daily, inevitable misunderstandings as they occur, not be surprised by them, but even learn to manage them! (Much of this book is designed to help you manage specific areas of your relationship.)

EVERY RELATIONSHIP GOES THROUGH PHASES

In addition to understanding that every couple will struggle, it is equally important to recognize that your relationship will go through phases, and some of the phases are more difficult than others.

Phase 1: Infatuation

Most relationships begin with infatuation. The Infatuation Phase is characterized by an increased heart rate, a "felt" excitement, and a tendency to see only the good in the other person. In this phase, the weaknesses of the other are minimized, perhaps not even seen at all! Each person seeks to please the other in big and small ways, for example, by giving a rose, opening a car door, buying gifts, or writing notes. During this phase, little is expected by the giver in return for what is given, and whatever is reciprocated is met with adulation! The energy expended in this first relationship phase comes naturally, with very little effort, and with a minimum of emotional drain. Love feels unconditional.

Phase 2: Reality

Then reality hits! At some point during the Reality Phase, both people begin to see the other person's faults and personality weaknesses. They are acutely aware of the other's selfish side, insensitivity, and noncaring behavior. They no longer see the other as Mr. or Miss Perfect. The bubble has officially been burst in this phase! Where once there was an increased heart rate, now the pulse is normal. Ideally, this phase occurs during courtship. But if they are married, it is during this stage that the wife secretly concedes, "I didn't marry a knight in shining armor, " and the husband reflects, "She may not be the girl of my dreams."

These stages will be a little different for everyone. Married couples have a responsibility to get through this phase. Single people have the option to reevaluate their relationship at this stage. Some people become so disillusioned during the Reality Phase that they break off the relationship. Many people never even get to the third stage of a successful relationship because they bail or step out at the Reality Phase.

Phase 3: Adjustment

The third and final phase of a loving or effective relationship is called the Adjustment Phase. At this point, both parties are committed to resolving their differences in mutually compromising and satisfactory ways. During this phase, acts of love are not always done because one feels like doing them, but because they are the right and loving things to do. In the Adjustment Phase the couple must put extra effort into doing things that came naturally to them in the Infatuation Phase.

During this final phase, the couple must be able to endure their pain and disappointments. In the Adjustment Phase, there is more focus on forgiveness, reconciliation, sacrifice, conflict resolution, and intentional listening. These acts of love will help the couple through a lifetime of relationship struggles.

CURRENT RELATIONSHIPS ARE AFFECTED BY OUR PAST

The third fact about relationships is that they are affected by our past. In most relationships, there is an area of conflict that occurs over and over. (Sometimes there are several areas!) When we examine the conflicting areas, we often find a person, crisis, or experience from our past that is affecting the way we are reacting in our current relationship. The influence from our past creates thoughts, feelings, or behaviors within us that can contaminate and damage our relationships. Some of these include distrust, insecurity, inadequacy, and fear of or the need to control.

For example, Bill has an outgoing and gregarious personality. He is very friendly, but at times almost overbearing. In his family of origin, he didn't receive much attention, encouragement, or affirmation. Therefore, as an adult, he has an insatiable need for approval, affirmation, and attention.

In his relationships with women, Bill's behavior appears to be flirtatious. He is unwilling to admit that this behavior is inappropriate, and he gets angry if his wife, Sue, mentions anything about it. Sue gives Bill a lot of attention, but that is not enough for him. His need for approval and affirmation keeps him searching for more attention.

Bill is attempting to fill a void that he feels inside, but his behavior is hurting Sue. He needs to understand that the effects of his past have created this insatiable need within him that has the power to damage his relationship with his wife. Because his compulsion to fill his void is so powerful, Bill loses perspective in all of his relationships.

Bill's need for more than normal amounts of approval, affirmation, and attention results in his flirtatious behavior. Sue doesn't appreciate his actions, and the effects of her past intensify her feelings of jealousy. Because Sue grew up not feeling special or significant, Bill's behavior hurts his wife more deeply than it would hurt most women (not that this behavior wouldn't hurt anyone). Because of her past, she struggles with strong feelings of insecurity and lack of love. His behavior frightens her. She chooses to withdraw from him to protect her feelings. He then receives less attention and searches for it even more in the wrong places.

Taking Practical Steps

You can take practical steps to overcome your past experiences.

1. The first step to take to better your current relationship is to become aware of the negative thoughts, feelings,

and behaviors that might be a result of your past. Check any from this list that might pertain to you:

- ☐ Need for unusual amounts of affirmation, affection, and/or approval
- ☐ Feeling rejected
- ☐ Being critical
- ☐ Not feeling valued, special
- ☐ Feeling abandoned
- ☐ Difficulty in trusting
- ☐ Hypersensitivity to anger
- ☐ Need to please
- ☐ Fearful
- ☐ Perfectionism
- ☐ Not feeling accepted
- ☐ Inadequacy
- ☐ Need to control
- ☐ Feelings of insecurity
- ☐ Secrecy
- ☐ Poor self-image
- ☐ Excessive spending

After you have identified a few of the thoughts, feelings, or behaviors on the list, recall the incidents from childhood that could have precipitated your reactions. To reflect on specific situations, you might want to set aside time to journal. During this time, write down the incident as you remember it. Include your feelings, thoughts, and reactions, as well as how the incident affected you. Then you can turn this reflection time into a prayer, asking God to help you forgive those who have hurt you and to bring healing to your past.

2. The second step is to acknowledge that your past experiences are hurting your present relationship. In doing this, you are helping your partner understand you better. Realizing that the current struggle is not just about the present circumstances diffuses the intensity of the current conflict. The admission and understanding of your weaknesses, as well as the influences of your past, lead to a greater sensitivity toward loved ones.

The following situation demonstrates how the past can hinder a current relationship. Joe hides his financial difficulties from important people in his life, especially his wife, Jane. He has purchased a number of items that he can't afford. These purchases put him in greater debt, but he doesn't want to share the severity of the situation with anyone, fearing that others might think he is inadequate and incompetent.

Joe's perception of himself as inadequate began as a child when he was ridiculed by his peers for being short and nonathletic. To counter his present inadequate feelings, he spends money excessively. Material possessions give him a sense of power and success. But his overspending has severely damaged his relationship with his wife because he has created a huge debt for them. He can no longer even provide necessities for her.

Hence the dilemma: Having been criticized in childhood, Joe developed a poor self-image and a feeling of powerlessness. As an adult, Joe numbs his pain by buying things, even though he can't afford them. Though spending money initially makes him feel powerful, it deeply and negatively affects his relationship with his wife. When Joe took the time to acknowledge that his past was affecting his relationship with his wife, it helped him to make some positive changes.

When we don't understand and resolve our past, we search for ways to cope with or numb our pain. The ways that we cope or numb can include the inappropriate use of money, sexuality, alcohol, drugs, or work. These can often and easily turn into addictions. In his counseling practice, Roger has found that most people with these addictions have unresolved family of origin issues. These unresolved issues can destroy marriages and families. *Understanding our past—and taking responsible steps to change—is fundamental to experiencing successful relationships.*

3. Another very helpful step we encourage you to take is to join a small group or support group. Roger and I have joined support groups, and we recommend the small group experience to you as well. Small groups and support groups are places where you can identify your issues and receive encouragement to work through them. Several friends attend Alcoholics Anonymous (AA), 12 Step groups, and growth groups. These groups differ from Bible study groups because they are designed to be places to honestly confess our shortcomings to one another.

The concept of attending small groups has been widely accepted in southern California for a number of years. Roger's friend, Ron Jensen, has developed and encouraged Spiritual Growth Groups, which focus on applying biblical principles in support group settings while at the same time providing accountability. Single and married men and women discuss the thoughts, feelings, and behaviors that hinder their relationships. In a safe setting, it has been remarkable to see how many men and women have been vulnerable, transparent, and willing to change.

EVERY RELATIONSHIP REQUIRES MOTIVATION TO SUCCEED

What motivates a couple or an individual to press on when confronting the truth about relationships? The knowledge that

- every couple is bound to struggle.
- every relationship goes through phases.
- current relationships are affected by our past.

What keeps both partners committed to each other during difficulty? What makes them fight for their relationship? What motivates a person to face the pain or disappointment in the relationship without giving up? Every person is motivated differently.

For some people, it is their *strong willpower*. They are actually motivated by their determination to never fail or quit. These people are often very disciplined and just won't accept failure. But self-will or inner motivation doesn't work for everyone. Some people have no trouble quitting. In fact, they often give up too soon.

Others are motivated to stay in a relationship for *fear of what people might think of them* if they ended a relationship, quit, or left. Although on the surface this doesn't appear to be a good motivator, it can have the positive effect of pushing the couple to discover better ways to relate to each other and avoid breakup.

Still other people are motivated to press through pain because of their *convictions* to keep their word. For example, if they went to the altar and said, "For better or for worse, for richer or poorer, until death do us part," they have made a verbal commitment in front of others and are determined to keep their promises.

Many are motivated to work through their pain because of their *spiritual commitments*. For example, some Christians stay married because they adhere to the biblical principles that "God hates divorce" and "what God has joined together, let no man separate." Their religious belief is their motivational factor.

Couples with children who are struggling in their relationship are motivated to resolve their differences for *the sake of their children*. They don't want their kids to be uprooted, moved to different homes, split up during the holidays, or forced to choose between parents. These people are driven to work out the difficulties in their relationship because they don't want their children to lose their sense of family, unity, stability, or security.

Having spent many years as a youth worker, Roger has seen and counseled hundreds of kids from divorced homes who have experienced incredibly painful feelings. He has watched as they were forced to make many difficult adjustments *simply* because their parents weren't motivated to persevere through the struggles in the Adjustment Phase of their relationship.

Certainly, where there is abuse or unfaithfulness, reconciliation is very difficult and a more complex process. But even in those cases, it might be possible, though much work will have to be done to save the relationship.

The following statements have been used to motivate married couples. Our hope is that by reviewing this list, you will identify thoughts that can motivate you to work through the struggles of your relationship.

1. It is unacceptable for us to fail.
2. I am determined not to quit.
3. I know that blessings will follow if I don't give up.
4. I might experience great pain if I stop trying.
5. I might leave a positive legacy if I just press on.
6. I might create great pain for my children if I leave now.
7. I probably will face this same problem with someone else in the future.
8. I am aware that nothing great was ever achieved without sacrifice.
9. I have the conviction of my own word.
10. All couples struggle; this is not abnormal.
11. I do not want to disappoint or let other people down.
12. My spiritual commitment will help me get through this difficult time.

Of course, there are less-noble motivations for remaining committed to a struggling relationship. Some people are paralyzed with the fear of facing the unknown, or they are unwilling to give up financial security supplied by the spouse. Though these motivations are not as healthy as others, they keep a couple together as they work through their struggles.

Wise People Seek Counsel

Perhaps even as you read this book, you feel too tired or discouraged to press on. You believe that you have done everything in your power to bring resolve. You've gone to counseling, prayer services, pastoral care, and therapy, and you've talked with friends—but nothing worked. If you are married, while we empathize with you, we must ultimately say, "Don't quit!" We believe that too many couples prematurely leave their relationship without considering the cost, or without turning over every rock possible to find resolve or resolution.

For those of you who have tried a counselor, yet haven't found help, try another. Get help, and get good help. If you are at an impasse, rather than give up, we suggest that you meet with a different professional Christian counselor or psychologist. Roger has seen many people receive help only after their fifth try! Sometimes the hearts take that long to soften. Perhaps one counselor is simply a better fit than another.

WHAT'S THE HONEST TRUTH ABOUT ALL RELATIONSHIPS?

We hope this chapter has helped you understand the following three truths about relationships:

1. Struggles are common to relationships.
2. All relationships go through phases.
3. Your past affects your present.

If you and your spouse can accept these truths and identify those things that will motivate you to stay committed to each other no matter what, it will make *living with them* much more satisfying.

■ *Chapter 2* ■

EVERY PERSON IS UNIQUE

When our son, Jacob, was born, I had just turned twenty-three years old. Though some women are very maternal, had younger siblings to care for, or loved to baby-sit in their teens, I have to admit, I had none of those attributes or advantages when it came to parenting. When I discovered that I was pregnant, I had never even contemplated how to nurture and care for a newborn. Therefore, from the first day of motherhood and with every visit to our pediatrician, I asked an array of simple, fundamental questions regarding child rearing. Because we were dealing with an entirely new stage in our lives, Roger and I were always monitoring Jacob's changes, growth, and statistics, concerned with his physical and developmental progress.

Our tendency was to compare him with other children to see if he was developing adequately. I continually asked his pediatrician, "How is Jake doing? Are his height and weight normal?" And every single time during the first six months of doctor visits, he gave me the same answer, "Avreebabeeindivijuva." Unfortunately, I couldn't understand that. Not wanting to appear impolite, I wouldn't ask him to repeat his answer, but I tried over and over in my mind to translate his words into English. I couldn't do it! Frustrated, I would go home and tell Roger, "I think the pediatrician is telling me that Jake is okay, but he keeps using a phrase that I don't understand. It sounds like this: 'Avreebabeeindivijuva.'" We were stumped!

I finally called my good friend Wendy, who also took her boys to the same small-town doctor. She just roared when I repeated the phrase! She, too, had been unable to understand our doctor at first, but she assured me that Jake was just fine. She told me that our wonderful pediatrician believed strongly that "every baby is an individual." During each visit, my doctor repeated that comment. He seemed determined to encourage us not to compare our child with another, but to celebrate his individuality! He wanted us to grasp the concept that *every child*, in fact, every person, is unique and different. This same concept needs to be understood when relating to the opposite sex.

UNDERSTANDING YOUR DIFFERENCES

Living compatibly with your spouse happens best when you accept, even appreciate, that there are differences. Most men think, act, and communicate differently from the ways women do. This is illustrated in John Gray's book *Men Are from Mars, Women Are from Venus* when he describes a man as a *cave dweller:* "Under stress he becomes very quiet and goes to his private cave to think about his problems. . . . When he has found a solution, he feels much better and comes out of his cave" (p. 30). Gray explains that a woman differs: "A woman under stress is not immediately concerned with finding solutions to her problems, but rather seeks relief by expressing herself and being understood" (p. 36).

Willard Harley's studies reported in *His Needs, Her Needs,* demonstrate that men and women differ in their needs. He found that most men ranked their top two needs as sexual fulfillment and recreational support, while women ranked affection and conversation as their top two needs (p. 10). These rankings don't hold true for everyone, but they show us that men and women are uniquely different.

Understanding our differences—in personalities and needs—can alter the way we think and act, making *living with them* more enjoyable.

DIFFERING PERSONALITIES

When we acknowledge that each person is born with a different personality, a different thinking process, and even different ways of responding to situations or doing things, we become more understanding of our differences. This knowledge ultimately allows us to accept others as unique rather than wrong.

We have found that the struggle to accept, tolerate, or change the other person's personality is one of the most common reasons that couples seek premarital and marital counseling. Roger regularly counsels those who have been trying to coerce the partner to perform, act, react, think, or be just like them! Especially his premarital couples express concern that they are not exactly like the person they are marrying. They often ask Roger, "Is it better for a couple to have the same or different personalities?" His response has been, "What is important to a successful relationship is not that you have the same personality, but that you . . .

> "1. Know *your own* personality type—which has both strengths and weaknesses.
>
> "2. Know *the other person's* personality type, with both strengths and weaknesses.
>
> "3. Make a conscious effort to focus on the other person's *strengths*.
>
> "4. Make a conscious effort to temper your *weaknesses.*"

Taking a Personality Inventory

In 1984, I attended my first Florence Littauer seminar. It was a speakers' training seminar called CLASS. Throughout the three days of instruction, Florence wove her material on personalities in and through the seminar. Her books and teaching, inspired by Tim LaHaye's book *The Spirit-Controlled Temperament*, explain human behavior in a simple, four-part temperament theory. For more than twenty-five years, Florence has been writing books and presenting seminars on personalities, and she has developed personality profiles and inventories so that people can understand themselves and others better.

Since my first introduction to Florence many years ago, Roger and I have attended a number of her seminars and shared her materials with hundreds of people.

Roger is convinced that a personality inventory is a "must use" tool for both premarital and marital counseling. He prefers the simplicity of resources from Florence Littauer, her husband, Fred, and their daughter, Marita. They have written excellent books on understanding personalities, such as *Personality Plus!* and *Personality Puzzle.* Their books discuss the four personality types, giving detailed descriptions of each category:

1. Sanguine (people who love to have fun)
2. Choleric (people who love to be in control)
3. Melancholic (people who must be meticulous)
4. Phlegmatic (people who are calm peacemakers)

We All Fall Within the Four Personality Types

Most of us have one predominant type and a secondary, less-dominant type. Though the "grass always looks greener on the other side," each person (and personality type) has an equal number of strengths and weaknesses. Therefore, it is not valid to refer to one personality as being better or worse than another!

The following list is a short inventory that will give you an idea of your primary personality trait. You may feel that you are predominantly one trait or an equal (or almost equal) blend of two traits. After looking at the list and short description that follows each trait, determine your primary and secondary personality types, then try to decide your partner's types. Enjoy a fun discussion about your traits, being sure to major on the other person's strengths and minor on the weaknesses.

The Fun Sanguine

Strengths	*Weaknesses*
1. Funny	1. Exaggerates
2. Life of the party	2. Dominates conversations
3. Entertainer	3. Self-centered
4. Optimistic	4. Disorganized
5. Energetic	5. Forgetful

If you are sanguine (fun and popular), you have the gift of conversation! You get along with most people and can talk to anyone and everyone. The downside of your personality is that you can very often be inconsistent, disorganized, and/or forgetful.

The Leader Choleric

Strengths	*Weaknesses*
1. Strong willpower	1. Can anger easily
2. Take-charge person	2. Overpowers people
3. Achievement oriented	3. Can't relax
4. Developer	4. Arrogant
5. Visionary	5. Domineering

If you are a choleric individual (leader), you want to be in control, but you have a tendency to be critical and intolerant of other, less-productive personalities. You are a decision maker, and often productive and profitable. But you have to be careful not to wound others with your words. You may need to extend more grace and mercy to other personalities!

The Serious Melancholy

Strengths	*Weaknesses*
1. Loyal	1. Tends to be a perfectionist
2. Organized	2. Prone to mood changes
3. Thorough	3. Lacks flexibility
4. Consistent	4. Less social
5. Sensitive	5. Shy

If you are a melancholy person (perfectionist, organizer), you enjoy structure, systems, and accountability. You are a faithful and loyal person. You see everything in black and white. While your strength is organization, your weakness is to be negative and critical.

The Easygoing Phlegmatic

Strengths	*Weaknesses*
1. Gentle	1. Worrier
2. Peaceful	2. Fearful
3. Calm	3. Procrastinator
4. Dependable	4. Indecisive
5. Thoughtful	5. Low energy

If you are a phlegmatic personality, you may need to push yourself to be more positive and decisive. You are sensitive and easygoing, easy to please, gentle, and flexible. You are the dependable type!

We believe that knowing personality types and traits is a real key to better understanding yourself and your relationships. This knowledge allows you to be more accepting, patient, and tolerant of others.

Difficulties with Differing Personalities

If your personality differs from your partner's, each must understand the other's strengths and weaknesses. Instead of trying to make the other person become like you, recognize that the different strengths balance your weaknesses! As you deal with personality issues, your goal is to focus on the positive personality traits of the other person.

If you're a parent, it is very important to be aware of all the different personality types in your family. If both parents are choleric or melancholy, the strength of your stricter personalities may cause your children to feel less loved. If you as a parent are aware of these differences, you can consciously make the adjustments to give more grace, mercy, and flexibility. If both of you are predominantly sanguine or phlegmatic, you will be less structured and therefore may need to develop organized systems to provide your children with greater structure.

In our marriage, Roger has the more phlegmatic (peaceful and calm) personality. So, while I appreciate that he is easy to get along with and will do what others want to do (more easily than I), he is also more reluctant to make quick decisions. When I begin to get irritated with his indecisiveness, I know I must immediately remind myself of his many strengths. This simple acknowledgment (in the form of self-talk or a reminder red flag that pops up in my mind) allows me to be more patient with him. (Note: Patience is not a strength of a sanguine/choleric; therefore, it takes a lot of self-control to do this!)

Of course, there are times when Roger becomes irritated with me! For instance, I have a bad habit of telling Roger that I know what he's thinking. I am convinced that he has some ulterior motive before he has a chance to explain his side of the situation. This really frustrates him because 99 percent of the time I'm incorrect in my assessment of his feelings, thoughts, and motives. When we slip into this pattern, he has to turn my sanguine quickness into calm discussion, which will allow him to express his true thoughts. When he gets irritated with me for my impatience, he reminds himself that this same trait makes me very productive.

Difficulties with Similarities

A couple came to us and shared their story. Before they got married, they felt great about their relationship! They had a lot in common, got along easily with each other, and seemed to enjoy doing most things together. Much to their surprise, after they were married, they found themselves often irritated and frustrated with each other. They soon realized that much of their difficulty arose because of their similar personalities.

They were both strong-willed, decisive leaders who were continually vying for power and control in their relationship. Since they hadn't previously recognized these strong personality traits, when the tensions and struggles occurred because of the similarities, they didn't know how to handle them.

One of the first exercises we gave them was a short personality inventory. They called us within the month to tell us that once each had clearly identified his or her own, then the partner's personality types and traits, they were surprised that their frustrations were based upon their many similarities (which were their strengths!). That insight, along with the decision to set guidelines and boundaries on the "who, what, when, where, and how" of using strengths, helped them get along better.

The Daily Test Drive

One particular activity sets Roger and me up for conflict because of our differing personalities. In this area, we are almost daily tested, tried, and challenged! An unofficial survey of our friends has assured us that this activity is a common area of conflict in most marriages. It is *driving*!

Roger's phlegmatic side takes over when he is at the wheel. He proceeds at a slow pace as if he had nothing else to do in life, nowhere to go, no schedule to keep. I, on the other hand, drive my car with one purpose in mind: to get to where I'm going as fast as possible by using all available shortcuts or time-savers! So while some may characterize my driving as an "Indy 500" style, they may describe Roger's style as the "slow boat to China."

When I am behind the wheel, Roger feels as if he should be wearing a helmet and racing suit. When he is behind the wheel, I feel like a turtle who is being passed by anything and everything. (But I'm not a quiet turtle, so I point to faster lanes, give directions to quicker routes, or comment about the bicycles passing our car!) Needless to say, these differences in our driving styles *on occasion* create tension.

In the past, I have tried to control myself by asking him if he knew the speed limit. By his look, he let me know that I had gotten too pushy. For the longest time, we continued to have tension over this difference, without finding a way to drive in the same car without fighting about the driving.

Finally, we consciously agreed that our personalities are different (and always will be) and that we drive differently (and probably always will!). We came to a point of accepting each other's style of driving and laid a few ground rules that could help us avoid some of the tension.

Here is what we've come up with: If I'm the driver, Roger just holds on for dear life. And though I've not gotten a speeding ticket in more than thirteen years, we have decided in advance that even if I get a ticket for speeding, I'll have to pay for it! When Roger is driving, he usually doesn't mind if I direct him to the place where we are going, but I can't tell him to switch lanes too many times or question him about how long it takes to get there! I have had to decide to enjoy the time with him instead of worrying about how fast or slow he is moving. (But if we're really in a hurry, I drive!)

Though these ideas may sound corny or even a bit out of balance, we talked through our differences until we could find out what worked for *us*. This is an important component to understand about personality strengths and weaknesses: What is satisfying for you, or what makes you happy, might be different from what works for other individuals or couples. Being willing to discuss your options, in light of your personalities, allows you to get along better with each other, especially in the areas of your differences that cause the most tension.

It is our strong conviction that becoming aware of your personality strengths and weaknesses, then making a conscious effort to focus on the other's strengths and modify your weaknesses will minimize your struggles or tensions.

We have seen couples with the exact same personality and those with almost opposite personalities get along wonderfully when they understood and adapted these concepts properly. (We recommend that you pick up a copy of Florence Littauer's book *Personality Plus!*, take the inventory, and study the book so that you can grow in your relationship together.)

Believe it or not, understanding each other's personality strengths and weaknesses is not the last thing you have to *know* in order to have a great relationship! Another significant concept in successful relationships is understanding that we also have differing needs!

DIFFERING NEEDS

The most common mistake we make is thinking that the other person's needs or desires are the very same as our own. We err in trying to meet the needs and desires of the other person because we base the needs on what we want rather than what the other person wants. The following example from our lives illustrates this point perfectly!

Because the fortieth birthday is such a big occasion, I wanted to give Roger something very special. Since I like to receive jewelry for special occasions, I thought I would buy a new wedding ring for Roger. His current ring was a plain, round, inexpensive gold band. I thought we should spruce him up with a brand-new wedding band! I found the perfect ring, but I asked the salesperson if I could return or exchange it if I bought the ring and Roger didn't like it. She assured me that it could be returned, so I purchased it, had it wrapped, and brought it home.

In front of our good friends and with great excitement, Roger opened the package. We all looked at him carefully to watch his response. He gave the look that says, "Oh, thank you for something that I don't really need or want!" But he didn't say those words.

I inquired, "Do you like it?"

"Well," he replied, "I like it, but I don't really need a new ring. In fact, I really like my old ring. It has sentimental value. I want to wear this until I die!" My heart sank, then it hurt. Then I got mad. (He told me later that he felt bad for not just accepting the gift with gratitude.)

What I learned that day, and admit that I have had to relearn a number of times since then, is that what Roger really wants or needs is not usually the same thing that *I* want or need. It's not even what I think he wants or needs! Guess what? We returned the ring and got him golf equipment that he really wanted.

Though there are exceptions, men and women don't *usually* have the same needs. It is more common for men and women to have *differing* needs.

In *His Needs, Her Needs,* Willard Harley proposes that you can "build or rebuild your marriage if you will learn to become aware of each other's needs and learn to meet them" (p. 9). One of Harley's strategies is to ask couples to rank their individual top five needs according to their importance. Through his research and surveys, he has identified the top ten needs of men and women:

1. Affection
2. Sexual relations
3. Conversation
4. Recreational companionship
5. Honesty and openness
6. Attractiveness of spouse
7. Financial support
8. Domestic support
9. Family commitment
10. Admiration (p. 197)

You might want to try the following exercise as a couple. From the list above, rank your top five needs, but don't reveal them to your partner. Next, take turns guessing what five needs the other person chose and rank the order of priority. Discuss who was able to predict the other's needs and priorities more accurately. Then, brainstorm ways that you could best meet each other's needs. The ultimate goal of this exercise is to focus on meeting your partner's top five needs.

Here's What Happened When We Tried Listing Our Needs

Roger listed recreational companionship as one of his top five needs. We talked about how I might meet that need. He shared that he would like me to golf with him, so we discussed *how often* he would like me to do that. I enjoy golf (when I'm killing the ball), but I don't like the fact that an eighteen-hole round of golf takes almost five hours to play. I shared that I would enjoy playing nine holes with him twice a month.

Rog shared that he would be happy if I would be willing to play at least nine holes with him, then he would finish the other nine on his own. He also wondered if *once in a while*, I would consider playing eighteen holes. I told him I could *occasionally* play eighteen holes, but not to expect that very often. Those options felt like a win-win to both of us, but I reasoned that to really *enjoy* golf, I needed to take some lessons to feel more confident and competent. I also thought I should get a better set of golf clubs in order to feel that I was getting a fresh start! Roger was so excited about my willingness to play golf that he helped me buy the best set of golf clubs that we could afford. That made me feel special, which also helped me get over my feeling that golf was a lot more work than fun. We both agreed, though, that if I tried hard to please him, but still harbored resentment about golf, we would try to figure out some other way to accomplish his need for recreational companionship.

I can't say that I always enjoy golf, especially when I perform the very technical moves called "whiff" and "duff." But because we have begun to enjoy the sport together, we find ourselves on a course or at a driving range on many evenings and weekends throughout the year.

Ultimately, Roger and I have found a fairly good balance in the area of recreational companionship. We enjoy doing some things together, but regularly enjoy different activities with other friends or family members as well. For example, Roger golfs with Ron Jensen once a week. In addition, he has a few other guys with whom he plays golf, including my brother. Consequently, his recreational enjoyment doesn't totally depend on me!

I consider companionship and recreation to be two different needs of mine. Because I am much more enthusiastic and committed to a cardiovascular (or aerobic) workout than Rog, I have not depended on Rog as a regular workout companion, though he *occasionally* does an aerobic workout with me. What I do need from Roger is a regular weekend date—or two! I love to go to movies, to plays, bowling, to sporting events, and out to dinner—as a couple or with others. I enjoy a full, fun weekend agenda *with* Roger, and for the past twenty years, he has graciously complied!

Taking the time to talk through your top five needs with each other, sharing what you can expect and what will be expected of you, can establish a healthy relationship! Even as you work through the actual meeting of these needs, you will almost always find that you need to make some adjustments, concessions, and sacrifices. Sometimes it will take a real effort.

In his popular book *Men Are from Mars, Women Are from Venus*, John Gray writes,

> Not only do men and women communicate differently but they think, feel, perceive, react, respond, love, need, and appreciate differently. They almost seem to be from different planets, speaking different languages and needing different nourishment.
>
> This expanding understanding of our differences helps resolve much of the frustration in dealing with and trying to understand the opposite sex. Misunderstandings can then be quickly dissipated or avoided. Incorrect expectations are easily corrected. When you remember that your partner is as different from you as someone from another planet, you can relax and cooperate with the differences instead of resisting or trying to change them. (P. 5)

We have found that a continual awareness of each other's differing personality traits and needs, and a conscious attempt to understand each other's needs and meet them, has made our relationship not only successful, but truly loving, happy, and fun. We are confident that if you strive to understand your partner's uniqueness, you will enjoy the very same success!

PART 2

THE SKILLS NECESSARY FOR SUCCESSFUL RELATIONSHIPS

■ *Chapter 3* ■

EFFECTIVE COMMUNICATION

Roger and I were nose-to-nose in the kitchen having what some call an argument, fight, disagreement, or tiff! We prefer to call it a miscommunication. It unfolded like this:

BECKY: I thought you told me you would be home at 7:00 P.M.

ROGER: No, I said that I'd be home at 7:30.

BECKY: I recall you telling me 7:00. I even wrote it down!

ROGER: Well, I put it in my calendar as 7:30.

BECKY: Okay. From now on, I'm going to tape-record our conversations because you never get it right.

ROGER: Good, because if you had tape-recorded our conversation, you would have heard me tell you I'd be home at 7:30.

BECKY: I don't think so.

These conversations can go *on and on* and never really seem to get resolved. They tend to spin us into more of a fury than they are worth! Our experiences with miscommunication or poor communication have often led to angry outbursts, stolen our intimacy, and truly hurt us in our relationship.

Conversely, effective communication has helped us to solve our conflicts. It has paved the way to peaceful resolution and has given us a closeness that we enjoy today.

In this chapter, we are going to look at three areas of healthy communication:

1. Rules for effective communication
2. Speaking the truth in love
3. Intentional listening

FOURTEEN RULES FOR EFFECTIVE COMMUNICATION

Before we frighten you with our *Fourteen Rules for Effective Communication*, we want to assure you that it is *normal* for every couple to develop poor communication habits, which after repetitive use can be very difficult to change or break! Our hope—and motivation—in encouraging you to establish *new rules* is twofold. First, we hope to assist you in changing your unhealthy communication styles, and second, we want to give you new and more effective ways to communicate with each other. The purpose of these rules is not to give you ammunition with which to control each other, but to give you a practical system designed to protect you from hurting each other. These rules thus serve as guidelines to follow when your emotions want to override, hinder, or stall your efforts at effective communication.

One last note: Roger has developed the fourteen rules for his counselees—and us—to live by! We have to admit that following these rules is not necessarily easy, especially if you have been communicating with other rules for any length of time. But we share them with great enthusiasm because when we have followed them, we have found them to work! Don't expect to change overnight, however. Be patient with yourself and your spouse. (We acknowledge that some of you might resist the idea of rules. If that is the case, we'd encourage you to think of the following list as tips or suggestions—for now. But eventually your goal should be to see these as ground rules to incorporate into your relationship.)

1. Don't Use the Words *Never* and *Always*

These words are used when you are frustrated or irritated, but they cause the other person to feel unfairly accused. When you use these words, you are usually exaggerating and not communicating precisely. Using the words *never* and *always* may communicate your frustration, but will hurt the other person by creating defensiveness. Here is an illustration:

ED: Debbie, would you go with me to the baseball game tonight?

DEBBIE: I have a lot of other things I need to do tonight. Besides, I really don't like baseball. It's kind of boring to me.

ED: I went with you shopping on Saturday, and I didn't really want to go. I *always* do what you want, but we *never* do what I want to do.

DEBBIE: That's not true! We don't *always* do what I want to do. Remember last week, when I asked you to go to a movie and we didn't go?

At this point, Debbie and Ed are no longer discussing or resolving the baseball game issue. They are arguing over *never* and *always*. These words actually get in the way of effective communication. Instead of *never* and *always*, use words such as *more* and *less*, or *often* and *seldom*, along with words such as *frustrated, irritated,* and *disappointed,* to communicate.

ED: Debbie, would you go with me to the baseball game tonight?

DEBBIE: I have a lot of other things I need to do tonight. Besides, I really don't like baseball. It's kind of boring to me.

ED: I'm disappointed because I feel as if I give in and do what you want to do more often.

2. Don't Blame, Shame, or Call Names

When you feel frustrated, hurt, or angry, you are tempted to strike back. You want the other person to feel what you are feeling. If you can blame or shame the other person, you think you will achieve a degree of satisfaction. But blaming and shaming statements cause both parties to feel miserable and will ultimately hurt the relationship. Avoid statements such as these:

- "You should have known better."
- "You are irresponsible."
- "It's all your fault."
- "There you go again."

Name-calling, labeling, and belittling are also extremely hurtful. Words such as the following fit into this category:

- *Idiot*
- *Stupid*
- *Jerk*
- *Irresponsible*
- *Lazy*
- *Selfish*

To belittle or name-call makes someone feel "less than." It is an attack on character and denotes disrespect. People remember these statements for a long time, and they are capable of causing much pain. To avoid name-calling, labeling, or belittling—as a rule used by both parties— makes the rule fair for both of you!

3. Use "I" Statements Rather Than "You" Statements

It is much easier to hear someone say, "I'm feeling frustrated," than to hear him or her say, "You frustrate me!"

"You" statements cause people to feel blamed or accused. They can no longer listen with empathy because their attention is focused on defending themselves. Therefore, "you" statements are counterproductive to healthy, effective communication efforts.

To not break this rule, you must become extremely conscious of your words and your emotions. Roger works very hard with his premarital couples to help them understand this concept, encouraging them to be aware of their choice of words. It is hard work, but avoiding "you" statements will enhance conflict resolution and improve your relationship.

Here are some examples of typical "you" statements, followed by a more appropriate "I" statement:

- "You make me angry when you come home late."
  "I feel upset because I was hoping that you'd come home on time."
- "You drive me crazy with your need to talk."
  "I feel a need for some private space each night."
- "You don't really care about our family."
  "I feel abandoned when I'm home alone."
- "You care only about your needs."
  "I feel sad because I don't feel that my needs are being met."
- "You don't care what this house looks like."
  "I don't like the house looking messy. I feel anxious when it's disorderly."

4. Say, "I Am *Hurt,*" Rather Than, "I Am *Angry* or *Mad*"

To increase your intimacy and decrease your aggression, you will want to reduce the number of times you use the words *angry* and *mad*. After you have been hurt in some way or another, it is a natural reaction to become angry. But more often than not, your *hurt* is your primary or root emotion. To communicate most effectively, you will want to express that root emotion. When you become frustrated, irritated, jealous, or hurt in some way, share *those feelings* rather than say that you are *angry*. When hurt is expressed, it leads to healing. But anger begets anger! Therefore, it is best to share your *hurt* rather than your *anger*. Chapter 4 will address the issue of anger control.

5. Take a Time-Out

If you become angry to the point of losing control or teetering on the edge of saying something purposely hurtful, we recommend that you call for a time-out. This technique protects your relationship from deteriorating further.

When our son, Jacob, was four years old and got upset and out of control, we told him to take a time-out. We asked him to go to his room for a few minutes to calm down. When he had settled down, he was able to handle his emotions more effectively. We have found that we are a lot like our son! We need to take time-outs so that we don't do major damage to our relationship by the words we say or the ways we react to stress. (You can read more about time-outs in Chapter 4 on anger control.)

6. Don't Withdraw or Isolate

When you withdraw or isolate, you hurt the other person. You create a situation where the other person feels ignored, cut off, or abandoned. Withdrawing can be perceived as a way to punish the other person. If you need to withdraw to stay in control of yourself, take a time-out, using the suggestions in Chapter 4.

7. Repeat to the Person What He or She Said to You *Before* You Share *Your* Thoughts, Feelings, or Possible Solutions

This process involves intentionally listening for the thoughts and feelings of your partner and then repeating them before sharing your thoughts and feelings. Acknowledging what the other person has shared is essential. First, it lets the other person know that you are listening intently, and he or she feels cared for. Second, it provides a way to check on the accuracy of what you heard. It keeps communication clear. This process is explained in greater detail in the section on intentional listening later in this chapter.

8. Don't Interrupt

Give the other person a chance to share. Interrupt only if you need to ask a question to better understand what is being said. It is especially difficult not to interrupt when you hear your partner saying things that hurt you.

Your natural tendency is to defend yourself. You may need to bite your tongue to keep from interrupting during these times, but forgo the temptation. You will need to tell yourself that you, too, will get a chance to share your feelings and thoughts, but you must wait until the other person is finished. We will discuss this topic in greater detail in the section on intentional listening.

9. Don't Demand

Rather than demand, ask! Demanding usually results in the other person's feeling controlled. Since most of us felt controlled by our parents as children, we don't respond well to demands. Demands can send shivers up our spines or even worse! It is much more effective to ask a question of the other person than to make demands. For example, ask, "Do you think you could . . . ?" or "Would you be willing to . . . ?"

10. Use the Phrase "I Would Like . . ." Rather Than "I Need"

Rather than say, "I need you to listen to me!" say, "I would like it very much if you would listen to me." To say, "I need," is to sound more demanding of a person. Though you may have a legitimate need, it is still better to communicate with a statement of desire.

11. Don't Use Threats

Threats can be detrimental to your relationship. You will have an instinctive tendency to use them when you feel hopeless, frustrated, or backed into a corner. Nevertheless, avoid threats at all costs. Call for a time-out, bite your tongue, but don't use threats. Threats are identified by the key word *if:*

- *"If* you don't stop nagging, I'll . . ."
- *"If* you ever do that again, I'll . . ."

Threats should be considered extreme measures that don't solve conflicts.

12. Be Affirming

Thank the other person for listening intently. But be sincere! Work very hard at keeping your communication positive. Even when you disagree with what your partner is sharing, you can still thank him or her for communicating thoughts and feelings. You can thank your partner for sticking with the conversation rather than isolating or withdrawing. Someone once told us, "It takes ten positives to balance out one negative," and we have found this to be true. Force yourself to communicate in affirming ways.

13. Never Use or Say or Ponder the "D" Word

When the heat gets turned up, and the frustration and anger begin to boil, you must be very, very careful to avoid saying things that will further injure your relationship. Using the word *divorce* has such adverse effects that it must be avoided at all costs. This word can pierce a person to the core. It can wound deeply and cause the other person to feel ultimate rejection and hopelessness. If you have used this word and haven't apologized, you should do so. If you have used the word and feel justified, you need to seek professional help. If there is physical abuse, infidelity, or alcohol or drug abuse, you must get outside help. It is impossible to have the intimacy required for a happy marriage in such circumstances.

14. Don't Use the Statement "You Broke the Rule"

These rules are designed to protect your relationship. Be careful not to use them to beat up or criticize each other. Rather than say, "You broke a rule," it is better to say something like this:

- "I felt hurt when you called me irresponsible."
- "I felt belittled when you told me I wasn't smart enough to understand that concept."
- "I felt defensive when you told me that I never cared about anyone but myself."

"You broke the rule" has a way of shaming the other person because it is a "you" statement rather than an "I" statement. It would be better to say, "I would like us to work as hard as we can to follow our rules. I feel that it really hurts us when we don't."

We acknowledge that rules, such as the fourteen you have just read, can be very simple to learn, but very difficult to follow! Some people keep them posted on the refrigerator to help them communicate more effectively. We will suggest other points to post such as anger control and a six-step plan to deal with conflicts. These can help you through challenging moments.

Points to Post

Fourteen Rules for Effective Communication

1. Don't use the words *never* and *always*.
2. Don't blame, shame, or call names.
3. Use "I" statements rather than "you" statements.
4. Say, "I am *hurt*," rather than, "I am *angry* or *mad*."
5. Take a time-out.
6. Don't withdraw or isolate.
7. Repeat to the person what he or she said to you *before* you share *your* thoughts, feelings, or possible solutions.
8. Don't interrupt.
9. Don't demand.
10. Use the phrase "I would like . . ." rather than "I need."
11. Don't use threats.
12. Be affirming.
13. Never use or say or ponder the "D" word.
14. Don't use the statement "You broke the rule."

If you knew us personally, you would know that if these rules were cumbersome or these guidelines were too strict, they just wouldn't "fly" in our home! Therefore, we submit the Fourteen Rules for Effective Communication as relationship enhancers, not relationship restricters.

Because we have used them in our home, and seen their power to bring about quicker resolution and fewer miscommunications, we are attempting to use them in all of our relationships, and we want to encourage you to do the same!

SPEAKING THE TRUTH IN LOVE

The instinctive reaction that humans have when faced with danger is called the "fight or flight" response. We either move toward or run from our attacker. We have the same "fight or flight" response when we communicate. When we feel threatened, afraid, or angry, we tend to react in one of two ways.

If your tendency is to lash out, attack, and become aggressive in your communication, you display the "fight" response. If you withdraw, back down, or isolate from attempting to solve conflicts, you lean toward the "flight" response. While there seems to be a natural inclination toward one reaction or the other, on certain occasions, each of us is capable of either response.

Proverbs 18:1–2 (NASB) aptly describes the "fight or flight" process:

■ ■ ■

He who separates himself seeks his own desire,
He quarrels against all sound wisdom.
A fool does not delight in understanding,
But only in revealing his own mind.

■ ■ ■

Verse 1 warns us against the "flight" response. When it speaks about separating oneself, it points out someone who withdraws or isolates, suggesting that the tendency is "against all sound wisdom." Rule #6: "Don't withdraw or isolate" addresses this issue.

Not communicating is just as ineffective as speaking harshly, unkindly, or overpoweringly. Verse 2 actually uses the word *fool* to describe someone who relies on the "fight" tactic. But if neither the "fight" nor "flight" response is a healthy way to resolve conflict, then what is the answer?

Early in our marriage, Roger and I found a verse in the Bible that provided a practical answer for us. In Ephesians 4:15 (NKJV) we discovered this phrase, "speaking the truth in love." (We even memorized it!) Within this verse we uncovered two principles that are necessary for effective communication.

The first principle is "speaking the truth." You cannot isolate or withdraw; you must speak if you are going to successfully resolve your differences and communicate your needs. In a healthy relationship, each person must be able to express himself or herself.

The second principle reveals that *how* you speak your words is just as important as *if and when* you speak them. The Bible teaches that effective communication is the fine art of expressing your words in a loving manner. Therefore, you should learn and practice the biblical concept of "speaking the truth in love." In fact, Roger believes that this verse teaches the same principle as present-day assertiveness training! Both systems encourage communication with assertiveness rather than aggressiveness. Assertiveness is a method of sharing your thoughts, ideas, or feelings truthfully and in a loving manner. Aggressive sharing speaks truthfully, but uses hostile words or methods.

Aggressive communication methods usually fall under the category of the "fight" response. The "fighter" may speak the truth but will miss the mark because the "love" factor is absent.

Still in Process!

I was getting ready to go on a bike ride with my friend Cindy. Rog was writing a portion of this book, working diligently toward the deadline. Because he was working and I was going to ride, we both felt tension.

Cindy came to the front door while I was still getting dressed. Roger was in his home office concentrating on the book, so I knew I shouldn't ask him to answer the door. Since no one answered the door after the first knock, Cindy knocked on the door again.

One more factor played into our situation. Our large, loud dog, Kezi, hadn't heard the first knock on the door. My son was sleeping, and Rog was working quietly, so if Kezi went into her protective mode and barked uncontrollably, it would definitely be disruptive. Yet I was still getting dressed. Thinking more about myself and not too deeply about the damage Kezi could do, plus feeling uneasy that Cindy was waiting at the front door, I sort of had a mental lapse and said, "Kezi, go see who's at the front door!" Kezi went into one of her four-alarm stages, barking loudly enough to wake the dead, and like the ninety-five-pound lady that she is, she bounded down the steps like a racehorse. Roger became totally frustrated, not to mention distracted.

How did we handle the "speaking the truth in love" principle? We failed! Roger yelled to me in a voice that was much more sarcastic than loving, "Can't you figure out what's going on?" He got the "speaking the truth" principle right, but missed the "love" connection.

Later on that morning, we apologized to each other. I admitted that I had really been inconsiderate, and I asked him to forgive me. He said, "Becky, I love you very much, and I'm sorry that I yelled. I was frustrated by the way you handled the situation. Do you think—next time—you could be more considerate of my desire to concentrate on the book and Jacob's need of sleep?" He genuinely spoke the truth in love!

We are committed to the principle "speaking the truth in love" on a daily basis. We have learned, and continue to be reminded, that neither withdrawing nor attacking is an effective way to communicate. A successful relationship will be established as people learn the skill of speaking in a loving manner.

INTENTIONAL LISTENING

We drive a Chevrolet Suburban. One of its shortcomings is that it doesn't provide adequate cup holders. While in a dealership, Roger simply mentioned to the service representative that he would have preferred a cup holder in the place of the CD holder.

We were quite surprised, one month later, to receive an unsolicited package in the mail from Chevrolet. Along with a cup holder, the enclosed note read:

Listening. It is an important activity as you appreciate nature—and as you appreciate your most important customers. Many of our

Chevy Suburban drivers have indicated they would like a cup holder in place of the cassette/compact disc holder. We appreciate your suggestions, and we act on them. Enclosed, you will find a specially designed insert which will enable you to rest beverages in the center console. (Instructions for its easy installation are included.) As one who appreciates nature and the Chevy Suburban, your input is always valuable in our quest to make Suburban an even greater companion on your adventures.

We were impressed with Chevrolet's desire to listen to customers with intent. Businesses that are effective and productive have learned that listening is a skill critical to customer satisfaction and, ultimately, to their long-term success. Successful couples have learned the same thing.

Listening Is a Learned Skill

In 1970, Roger finished his first master's degree in counseling. The program was one full year of learning how to listen. At that time, Carl Rogers brought listening to the counseling forefront as the key to helping people. Also in the 1970s, Thomas Gordon, author of *Parent Effectiveness Training,* coined the phrase "active listening." And more recently, author and seminar speaker Harville Hendrix promotes listening with the term *mirroring.* But more than two thousand years ago, the Bible talked about listening in this way: "He who answers before listening— that is his folly and shame" (Prov. 18:13 NIV). This verse is referring to the trouble one finds himself or herself in when one doesn't listen with the intent to hear *and* to understand the other person.

Since Roger began his counseling career, he has used and taught listening as a basic communication skill necessary for any healthy relationship. We call his process *intentional listening,* which involves three basic steps for each person to go through. (First, we will explain the process. Then we will illustrate all the steps.)

Step One: Listen with awareness. In this initial step, the goal is to listen intently to what the other person is saying. In the listening step, one must focus on listening for certain things specifically. The specifics should include both the thoughts and the feelings that the other person is articulating. You listen with empathy to what the other person is saying by paying attention to feelings. You attempt to understand the other person by listening to the thoughts.

The real trick in Step One is to make a conscious effort to reserve your emotions and comments, rebuttals and excuses, for another time. This will be difficult, so in the Fourteen Rules for Effective Communication, Rule #8: "Don't interrupt" should be followed. *The purpose of Step One is to grasp the other person's thoughts and feelings.*

Step Two: Paraphrase what you heard. The purpose of repeating or paraphrasing what the other person says is to help him or her feel listened to, cared for, and understood.

In the awareness step, you listened with the intention of understanding the other person's *thoughts.* When you listened for expressions of feelings, you were empathizing. The process of Step Two is to paraphrase or repeat those *thoughts and feelings* to the person. (Remember this is Rule #7: "Repeat to the person what he or she said to you *before* you share *your* thoughts, feelings, or possible solutions.")

The paraphrasing step means that the listener rewords the other person's thoughts, identifying and articulating what the listener believes the other person is thinking and feeling. During this step, repeating verbatim what the other person said can be an effective method unless this method causes the other person to question your sincerity or empathy. In that case paraphrasing would be better. It is important to find each person's level of comfort in this step.

Once you have articulated to the other person your paraphrased version of the thoughts and feelings, Step Three naturally follows.

Step Three: Inquire. **Question #1:** After paraphrasing the thoughts and feelings you have heard, you must ask, "Did I understand you correctly?"

Most often, the listener leaves out a thought or feeling, or misinterprets something in the paraphrase step. The inquire step gives the other person a chance to clarify or correct your paraphrased version of the thoughts and feelings.

Believe it or not, you're not finished with Step Three! There are three questions in Step Three. In the first inquiry, you ask if you understood the thoughts and feelings *correctly*.

Question #2: Ask, "Is there anything more you would like to share about this?"

Question #3: The third question in Step Three occurs when the one who shared first says, "Thank you for listening to me. Is there anything you would like to share about this situation?"

When you finish Step Three, repeat the process of listening with awareness, paraphrasing, and inquiring for the other person.

Note: This explains the process of intentional listening. A normal transition at this juncture would be to ask for and extend forgiveness. As difficult as intentional listening may be, the forgiveness process is equally difficult and will be explained in Chapter 5.

A Tirabassi Illustration of the Intentional Listening Process

Roger and I went over to the driving range one afternoon to hit a bucket of balls. Believe it or not, this fun activity created a conflict for us! Because the grass on the driving range had been chipped and pitched and driven into dust, we found ourselves with very few positions from which to hit off green grass. After we had both hit a bucket of balls, I pulled up a lawn chair and began to watch Roger hit.

At this range, a yellow cord is used as a boundary line to keep golfers from hitting off new grass. I noticed that Roger was hitting behind the yellow cord instead of in front of it. I said, "Rog, what are you doing?" He gave me a puzzled look as if to say, "Why? What is wrong with what I'm doing?" I spoke my thoughts and quipped, "You're not allowed to do that." He replied, "Sure I am." We carried on this disagreement in various forms until we had packed up and gotten into the car, at which point (possibly because we finally had privacy) Roger said, "I feel frustrated when you make such a big thing over something that is insignificant."

Our differences were causing our emotions to escalate. At that juncture, we stopped ourselves from heading down that path and agreed to enter into the *intentional listening* process.

BECKY: We obviously disagree on the significance of this issue. Can I tell you how I feel about this?
ROGER: Sure.

(Step One)

BECKY: If you want to hit a bucket of balls from behind the yellow cord when I'm not with you, go ahead. But I feel it is socially inappropriate, even embarrassing, and I would prefer you not do it when I'm with you.

(Step Two)

ROGER: So you think that this is inappropriate and you would feel better if I didn't hit behind the line when you are with me.

(Step Three, Question #1)

ROGER: Did I understand you correctly?
BECKY: Yes. But I also felt embarrassed.
ROGER: So, in addition, you felt embarrassed?

BECKY: Yes, that's right.

(This leads to Question #2.)

ROGER: Is there anything more you would like to share about this?

BECKY: No. That's all I was feeling and thinking. (This leads to Question #3.) Thank you for listening to me. Is there anything you would like to share about this situation?

(Step One)

ROGER: Well, to me, this was not such a big deal. It seemed obvious that there were no more green, grassy spots and that they were going to have to move the yellow cord back within the day. I'm over there a lot and didn't feel as if what I was doing was offensive to anyone. But I do want us to enjoy our time together at the driving range, so I will respect your feelings and not hit from behind the yellow line when you are with me.

(Step Two)

BECKY: So, you think it is okay, and you feel comfortable to hit behind the yellow cord at the driving range since you are there a lot. But you understand my feelings and won't do that when we're together, especially because you want us to feel good about going to the driving range together.

(Step Three, Question #1)

BECKY: Did I get that right?
ROGER: Yes. That is how I feel about it.

(Question #2)

BECKY: Is there anything more you want to share?

ROGER: Yes, I love you! (Kiss, kiss!) Thanks for listening to me!

(This ends Step Three.)

Why is *intentional listening* so hard to master? The main reason is that the listener's *emotions* get hooked. In this example, when I told Roger he wasn't allowed to hit from behind the yellow cord, I hooked his emotions. He felt criticized, so his tendency was to defend himself. In most situations, without the commitment to *intentional listening*, Roger would be tempted to respond with his thoughts and feelings instead of focusing on my frustrated feelings.

Most of us face the same temptation. Our individual hurt feelings and emotions will desperately try to get free and be expressed immediately! We must remember this process calls for the listener to *initially* restrain emotions and listen with the intention of understanding the other person's thoughts and feelings. If the other person knows that he or she will have a chance to respond, as well as have an opportunity to become "the listener," it makes it easier to listen completely. The goal of *intentional listening* is to avoid becoming defensive or overreacting when your feelings get triggered.

REVIEWING THE SKILLS OF
EFFECTIVE COMMUNICATION

To be successful in relationships, we need to communicate with ground rules that level the playing field, speak the truth in love and, when there is tension, quickly resort to using intentional listening techniques.

Roger and I have found that the most effective communication occurs when our relationship is a safe place to have a two-way conversation where we can share our hearts and hurts without hurting each other.

■ *Chapter 4* ■

ANGER CONTROL

Anger in itself isn't bad. It is a normal feeling that we usually experience several times a day. We need to become aware of it and accept it as essential, but learning how to control it so that we avoid destructive experiences is equally important. Anger doesn't hurt relationships, but how we express that anger can be very detrimental to our relationships.

If you are at all like us, anger control is an extremely difficult skill to master. When someone says or does something that causes us to feel hurt, irritated, or frustrated, we can easily lose control. Our angry, out-of-control *reactions* have the potential to cause as much or more damage than the initial action! Loss of control of our words, nonverbal expressions, or our actions can destroy our relationships.

UNDERSTANDING ANGER

Anger is usually a secondary emotion experienced in frustrating situations. There is usually a root emotion that we experience first. In *The Angry Man*, David Stoop and Stephen Arterburn identify some of these root emotions as frustrations, guilt, fear, grief, and confusion (pp. 55–63). Mary Ellen Donovan and William P. Ryan in *Love Blocks* state it this way: "Whenever there is anger, it usually is a reaction to another, deeper feeling and serves as a way of covering that feeling up" (p. 324).

Expressing Your "Hurt" Rather than Your Anger

Again, before we become angry, we typically experience some form of hurt. The "hurt" may stem from feeling rejected, misunderstood, or neglected, or not feeling cared for or important. Instead of expressing our hurt feelings of sadness or disappointment, or our fears of rejection, we more commonly lash out in anger.

Donovan and Ryan assert, "The most common messages behind a stance of 'I am angry,' are 'I am hurting,' 'I am depleted and in need of love and affection,' and 'I feel unappreciated and unloved.' But when anger is expressed in lieu of these underlying feelings, it has precisely the opposite of the desired effect" (p. 325).

If you initially share those hurt feelings with the other person instead of the fact that you are angry, you have a better chance to avoid a fight and start the healing process. When you tell the other person that you are angry at him or her, you are usually met not with sympathy or an apology, but with anger.

When a person says he or she is angry with you, you may feel inadequate, guilty, judged, or hurt. A cycle from anger to hurt to anger will follow. Expressing "hurts" moves you out of the anger cycle and into the healing cycle. In Chapter 3, we discussed Rule #4: "Say, 'I am *hurt*,' rather than, 'I am *angry* or *mad*,'" as a practical way to get out of the anger cycle and move into the healing cycle. We have found that it is much more effective to communicate our hurt and pain rather than our anger, hate, or resentment.

Here's an example:

DAN: Mary, I'm so angry at you. I hate it when you tell me to pick up my clothes three times in a half hour!

MARY: Well, I'm angry at you too. If you are going to act like a child, I'll have to treat you like one!

In this example, Dan's expression of anger increased Mary's tendency to defend herself rather than helped her understand Dan's feelings. In fact, she resorted to anger.

Let's look at a better way for Dan to express himself when he is being criticized:

DAN: Mary, I feel as if I'm your child when you ask me to pick up my socks three times in a half hour. I feel hurt and humiliated.

MARY: I get irritated because I feel as if I need to pick up after everyone every day! I don't want to make you feel humiliated, but I do need help.

Because Dan shared his hurt feelings rather than his anger, Mary was less defensive, yet still able to share *her* hurt feeling of not being supported. This exchange of "hurts" diminished the negative effect that anger would have on this situation. This concept is hard to put into practice because we are more prone to jump right into the expression of anger than to share our initial hurt feelings, but it is worth the effort.

In Roger's work with couples, he often has to stop and correct them until they begin to share their hurt feelings instead of their anger. At first, this process feels unnatural because most of us have developed the habit of communicating in a defensive, angry manner. As the intensity of the hurt increases, the intensity of the anger also increases, which is why it takes an incredible amount of self-control to communicate the hurt first.

It's Not So Much What You Say, but How You Say It

Saying things harshly or being impatient often starts things going in the wrong direction, which results in other things going wrong. Proverbs 15:1 reveals the pattern: "A gentle answer turns away wrath, / But a harsh word stirs up anger" (NASB). At this point, most relationships begin to spiral downward. We become hurt and angry over one incident, and another incident follows right behind. This triggers more frustration. If we aren't careful, we can react in even more unhealthy ways with harsher words, inappropriate withdrawal, and less loving actions. In other words, things escalate.

When we are not able to control the words that come out of our mouths, we can severely hurt our relationships. It is no secret that some people have a more difficult time restraining their words than other people do. Very often, those who have been brought up in families where there was little restraint develop similar habits that are difficult to break.

Proverbs 22:24–25 tells us: "Do not associate with one easily angered, / or you may learn his ways and get yourself ensnared" (NIV). Practically speaking, if you grew up in an angry family, you will most likely struggle with this problem. To overcome the tendency to become easily angered, you must work extra hard *on a conscious level* to control your words. In addition, it is helpful to reflect on your past and remember how damaging an effect those outbursts and unrestrained words might have had upon you. It is imperative that you make a solid resolution to avoid such behavior. Admitting that you struggle with anger and asking for forgiveness when you fail in this area are two essential steps for the preservation of your relationships. To change your behavior, you may need to forgive those who have hurt you by the hostile expression of their behavior.

Bite Your Tongue

Controlling *what* you say and *how* you say it is a key to maintaining a successful relationship. It might mean that you have to literally bite your tongue in order *not* to say something that could further damage the relationship. Ideally, you should plan in advance how to deal with the strong emotions that have previously propelled you into dangerous verbal expression. A practical plan or system, by which you can avoid reverting to dangerous verbal attacks, should include adhering to rules that protect your relationship from abuse or whispering to yourself memorized statements, such as, "What the other person is saying to me right now is hurting me, but I will have a chance to share my thoughts and feelings when he or she is finished."

When Roger and I are in a conflict, we often struggle to allow the other person to express complete thoughts, and frequently we interrupt. When our feelings get stepped on, we lash out quickly with our own defense or criticism. Without positive conscious thoughts, we end up blurting out counterproductive statements.

Take a Time-Out

Besides biting your tongue and memorizing conscious thoughts, having a time-out is an effective way to get control. You take a time-out to get *yourself* under control, thus protecting yourself from doing any more damage to the relationship! In fact, there should be a prescribed way of taking a time-out, because if it is not taken at the right time or in the right way, even a time-out can be detrimental to your relationship.

Once again, you take time-outs to get *yourself* under control and to protect the relationship. Therefore, time-outs are not taken by abruptly walking away or for unspecified amounts of time. Those actions are considered withdrawal, not time-outs.

The most effective way Roger and I have found to take a time-out is to say to the other person, "I'm feeling the need to take a time-out. Could we come back and talk in a half hour?" The goal is to let the other person know that you are not trying to withdraw from, hurt, or abandon him or her, but to get yourself in a better emotional state in order to resolve the conflict. It is important to agree to come back at a specified time, perhaps in thirty minutes to an hour. The time frame can be flexible, but both parties must agree upon it.

SIX QUICK STEPS TO CONTROL YOUR ANGER

We have compiled a practical list of *six quick steps* that can help you control your anger. The goal is to put them in daily view and use them as an immediate resource for anger control when you feel the first strong wave of emotion coming over you.

1. Notice the Physical Warning Signs

Anger can be a very dangerous emotion with physical manifestations: (*a*) red, hot cheeks; (*b*) tense muscles; (*c*) glaring eyes; (*d*) increased pulse; (*e*) heavy breathing; (*f*) burning or seething in your chest; and or (*g*) nausea. All of these characteristics are built-in red flags. They are warning signs, so tell yourself that you can do *major* damage to your relationship when you experience them. The sooner you notice them, the quicker you will be able to step away from an inappropriate, out-of-control reaction and move toward a less-emotional response or reaction. *Pay attention* to these physical signs. See them as helpful, God-sent protective indicators!

2. Take a Deep Breath

Take two or three deep breaths to calm yourself. Then, when you have the opening, communicate without hostility. By taking a few deep breaths to relax yourself, you'll be able to calmly share your thoughts and feelings without using harsh words and/or increased volume.

3. Decide Not to Attack

Get your anger under control by counting to ten or to one hundred, but *don't attack* the other person emotionally or physically! Take a time-out if necessary, but don't attack. Bite your tongue if necessary, but don't attack. *Pray*. Keep on praying, but don't attack. The goal in controlling your anger is to not say or do anything until you can calm yourself enough to think more rationally. Saying the wrong thing or using angry, impulsive words could potentially do more harm to the relationship than the initial problem.

4. Whisper Calming Statements to Yourself

To prepare yourself for times when your anger wants to take over, memorize statements you can whisper to yourself, for example:

- "What the other person is saying to me right now bothers me, but I will get a chance to share my feelings and thoughts when he or she is finished."
- "I don't need to explode—I can say what I am feeling in a calm way."
- "I must season my speech with grace."

- "I will be able to deal with this when I calm down."
- "I can do permanent damage if I let myself lose control."
- "I am hurting, but I am going to be okay."

5. Remind Yourself That You Are Accountable to Someone

Telling one or a number of people that you are striving to use discipline and self-control in the area of anger (outbursts, reactions, tone of voice, etc.), and asking them to continually (daily if necessary) ask you how you are doing, can really help you not to lose control. Knowing that you have to face them, tell them, confess, or admit failure to them may be the only reason that you do not lose control. I know this works because I have tried it!

6. Identify the Hurt (and Express It When You Are in Control)

Search for the true feelings that have caused the anger. Remember, anger follows hurt. So ask yourself, Do I feel inadequate, judged, not important, jealous, used, abused, lonely, hopeless, helpless, worthless, guilty, or afraid? Ask yourself, Where am I hurting?

REMEMBER . . .

Controlling your anger is one of the most loving things you can do for your partner. Expressing your hurt rather than your anger, avoiding a harsh or impatient tone, biting your tongue or taking a time-out when necessary, and following the six quick steps to controlling your anger will make you a joy to live with!

Points to Post
Six Quick Steps to Control Your Anger

1. Notice the physical warning signs.
2. Take a deep breath.
3. Decide not to attack.
4. Whisper calming statements to yourself.
5. Remind yourself that you are accountable to someone.
6. Identify the hurt (and express it when you are in control).

■ *Chapter 5* ■

FORGIVENESS

One of our favorite television programs is *Home Improvement*, with Tim "the Tool Man" Taylor. Over the past few years, we've been impressed with Tim's openness to better his marriage. He regularly seeks relationship advice from his neighbor, Wilson, and he even willingly (or was it reluctantly?) attended group counseling. And with each passing year, he apologizes more often and quickly than the year before!

Our favorite episode is the one in which Tim acknowledges that he has an obsession with automobiles. After hot-wiring his wife's car because she didn't want him to drive it, he got caught! His neighbor, Wilson, suggested that Tim do the "right thing" and ask her to forgive him for all the times he had treated cars as if they were more important than she was. The following discussion was the result:

TIM: I want to apologize for all the times I wronged you automotively.

JILL: That could take years.

TIM: I need help. I'm thinking of checking into the Henry Ford Clinic.

It was a cute illustration showing: (1) that couples repeatedly struggle in certain areas, and (2) that couples have a continual need to ask for and extend forgiveness!

Most people will agree that forgiveness is an essential relationship skill, but they struggle with how to give and receive it. In other words, they believe in forgiving, but get stuck when trying to do it.

Roger and I believe that forgiveness is a fundamental act of love that we can extend to each other on a daily basis. Hardly a day goes by that we don't—in some form or fashion—hurt each other.

Although we try not to, we sin every day. Our impatience, procrastination, selfishness, pride, competition, jealousy, greed, fears, lusts, laziness, and anger are all ways that we hurt each other. We rarely go a day that we don't need to ask for or extend forgiveness toward each other.

Forgiveness is defined in *Webster's Dictionary* as "canceling a debt, or granting pardon for an offense or sin." When we truly forgive, we choose to endure the hurt and pain, and let the other person off our hook. We decide not to get even because to get even means we haven't truly forgiven. When we forgive, we decide *not to do unto them what they did unto us!*

Two aspects are involved in the forgiveness process: (1) asking for forgiveness, and (2) extending forgiveness.

ASKING FOR FORGIVENESS

In our relationship, we have found that there are differing levels of pain that we inflict upon each other. Some of our actions hurt the other person deeper than other actions and thus require more sensitivity in seeking forgiveness. Here are three levels of infraction, and corresponding ways to ask for forgiveness at each level.

Level 1: Minor Infraction

When the infraction is minor, it seems rather easy to say you are sorry. In these situations, there is less anger or emotion to work through. When the irritation has less magnitude, and there is not a great deal of hurt, it is still important to say you are sorry *and* ask for forgiveness. Roger and my *minor infractions* occur over the following:

- The television clicker—who gets to control it?
- Should we turn on the car air-conditioning or open the windows?
- Should the dog be walked by me or us? (And whose dog is she anyway?)
- Who should go through the pile of mail?
- Who should water the lawn?

Level 2: Misdemeanor

The second level is a *misdemeanor*. Unlike a minor infraction, this level has more emotion attached to it. Whatever you have done to hurt the other person has definitely upset him or her. Not only should you say you are sorry, then ask to be forgiven, but you should also verbalize *how* you have specifically hurt the other person.

Here are examples:

- "I'm sorry that I left you alone at the party for a longer amount of time than you were comfortable. I was being selfish, trying to fit business into the evening. Will you forgive me?"
- "I'm sorry that I forgot to pick up the dry cleaning, especially after I told you this morning that I would do it to save you the trip. Will you forgive me?"
- "I'm sorry that I fell asleep last night after I told you we would make love. Would you please forgive me?"

Embarrassing your partner and being inconsiderate, selfish, or late are other infractions that fall under the misdemeanor category. In this level, the offended person feels uncared for or unimportant. It is your goal, as the offender, to admit your insensitivity, then comfort and care for your partner.

Level 3: Felony

We call the deepest level of infraction a *felony*. You are in big trouble when you mess up on this level! When you commit a felony, you are not likely to get an "I forgive you" the first time around. You may have to come back a few times before you receive forgiveness. It may take a few hours *if you are fortunate*! This infraction causes the deepest hurt. The offended person usually feels degraded, demeaned, rejected, attacked, betrayed, or intentionally hurt. You need to show sincere sorrow if you have committed a felony. In addition, you will need to develop a plan to prevent the situation from happening again.

Consider some examples of felonies:

- Using the word *divorce* to hurt your mate
- Using hurtful words that are deeply wounding to the other person (such as, "You're just like your mother!")
- Committing acts that cause deep distrust
- Causing rejection or abandonment feelings in the other person

A Tirabassi felony. One morning we were in bed talking and disagreed about how we were handling our workloads. The more we talked, the more we disagreed. We both felt frustrated, and the annoyance mounted. It was one of those escalating disagreements that got out of control. Roger ended up comparing me to someone else. His statement was very hurtful to me. He knew he was out of control, but he wasn't able to stop himself. The damage was done. The room was quiet. I needed to leave the room to regain my composure, and so did he. He tried to apologize, but I wasn't ready. I was too hurt by his cutting remarks.

It was a warm morning, so I went out to the backyard to calm myself, read my Bible, and try to pray. Roger came to the backyard and said he was sorry for his remarks, but I didn't respond to him. He knew how hard the remarks had hit me, so he backed off. He said he was sorry, and he knew that I needed time.

He came back two or three times, but I still wasn't ready. His words had left a deep wound, and no matter how hard I tried, I couldn't seem to find a sense of peace. After some reflection, prayer, and processing of the whole situation, I said I was ready to talk. He began the conversation by saying, "Becky, I'm so very sorry for this morning, and for the personal comparison that caused you so much pain."

He allowed me to share my pain and thoughts, then repeated them to me. He added, "I'm sorry for causing you to feel humiliated. I'm sorry that I hurt you so much. I was wrong for saying those words."

I shared honestly that it really devastated me to think that the person who loves me most would hurt me so deeply. I added that those types of statements (comparisons, degrading remarks, etc.) make it difficult for me to trust him.

Roger then said, "I would like you to forgive me, but I know it might take time. I want you to know that I was too emotional and should have calmed myself. I didn't mean what I said. I said it in anger, which was wrong. I'd like to ask you to forgive me. If you can't, I'll wait. I also want you to know that I will not say those words again to you." I forgave Roger, and I also asked him to forgive me for my part.

Reviewing the Levels of Infraction

Though asking for forgiveness at the first level, minor infraction, often involves a light, even humorous, tone, the next two levels, misdemeanor and felony, require us to follow important guidelines for appropriately communicating our sorrow to and asking for forgiveness from the one we have hurt or offended.

A level 1 apology begins with a very short, simple statement in which we ask for forgiveness. This is most effective and usually very acceptable for very minor offenses. A level 2 apology involves increased detail, appropriate to the degree of pain that was caused. At level 3, we are dealing with a deeper degree of hurt or pain. In these situations, we need to communicate a deeper degree of sorrow for hurting the other person, and allow more time for him or her to extend forgiveness. Following are sample apologies appropriate for each level:

Level 1: Minor Infraction: "I'm sorry for hurting you. Will you forgive me?"

Level 2: Misdemeanor: "I'm so sorry for hurting you and making you feel and think _____ _____. Will you forgive me?"

Level 3: Felony: "I'm so sorry for hurting you by _____ _____ (*my actions*) _____ and making you feel and think _____ _____. I am in need of forgiveness. I would like to do whatever I can to make it up to you. Is there anything I can do? Do you think you could find it in your heart to forgive me?"

EXTENDING FORGIVENESS

Having illustrated how to ask for forgiveness, now we need to discuss the task of extending or granting forgiveness. Forgiving someone for hurting you can be a difficult assignment. Obviously, some "hurts" are easier to forgive than others. Usually, the degree of difficulty in forgiving others corresponds to the intensity of the hurt experienced. It is not too hard to forgive someone for minor infractions, but when you experience a deep pain, or the same pain over and over, forgiveness doesn't come easily.

Here are some helpful motivators to assist you in forgiving others:

1. *To forgive someone benefits you.* To forgive someone is to do yourself a favor. When you don't forgive, you hold on to bitterness and resentment. If you allow bitterness to fester, you may become a very irritable, unhappy, bitter person. A friend once told me, "I realized that by not letting them off the hook, I was really the one on the hook! Once I forgave them, I was free."

2. *To forgive doesn't mean you allow the person to continue to hurt you in the same way.* To grant someone forgiveness doesn't mean you allow the person to continually hurt you. You should establish boundaries to protect yourself from a repeated situation. For example, you were hurt when a person you trusted didn't maintain confidentiality. On several occasions, he or she told other people what you had confided. After realizing the pain caused you, he or she apologized. You should extend forgiveness to him or her, but in the future, you might decide not to confide in him or her. We encourage you to forgive, but to take specific steps to protect yourself in the future.

3. *Most people don't intentionally try to hurt you.* Many times people hurt you because they see a situation differently from the way you do or because they are hurting inside. They are more in touch with their feelings and less aware of what you might be feeling. While that insensitivity hurts you, knowing it was not intentional makes it easier to forgive them.

4. *God wants us to forgive others.* Throughout the Bible, we learn that God is interested in reconciling relationships. He forgives us so that we can be reconciled to Him. He is so serious about this principle that He says, "If you do not forgive men their sins, your Father will not forgive your sins" (Matt. 6:15 NIV). This biblical principle is designed to motivate us to extend forgiveness to others!

5. *It won't be long before you will need to be forgiven.* In every close relationship that Roger and I have, it has been our experience that before long we cause the other person pain. The chances are good that we will need to be forgiven by the very person we are struggling to forgive. Being mindful of this possibility can motivate us to forgive quickly. The biblical principle that assists us is, "Judge not, that you be not judged" (Matt. 7:1 NKJV).

What Roger and I have repeatedly experienced is that whenever we become critical with the other person for something he or she has done wrong, we make the same error before the day, week, or month is up! Once again, this knowledge keeps us humble and more willing to offer forgiveness.

6. *Forgiveness becomes easier when you look for similar behavior in your life.* Admitting that you have also hurt others makes it easier to forgive others. A verse that warns us against judging is also applicable in helping us forgive more easily: "Why do you look at the speck of sawdust in your brother's eye and pay no attention to the plank in your own eye?" (Matt. 7:3 NIV).

More than anyone else, Roger's friend Ron Jensen has helped him to understand this biblical principle. When men get together, they frequently discuss how their wives irritate them. In the past, Ron and Roger engaged in such conversations, which might have sounded like this:

MAN 1: Yesterday was a terrible day. My wife was all over me for not paying attention to her. She's forever criticizing me for something.

MAN 2: I know what you mean. My wife gets on me too! She's always harping on me about something or other.

This is what some would call "typical man talk." Since focusing on the Matthew verse about the plank and the speck, however, Roger and Ron have determined to disallow this "typical man talk" in their relationship. If Roger attempts to criticize me, Ron doesn't let him get away with it! (I think Ron's great!) The minute Roger starts to complain about me, Ron will say, "What does that have to do with *you*, Rog?" In other words, "Where is the plank in your own eye? What is it about *you* that you disapprove of in Becky?"

It becomes easier to forgive others when we realize that much, if not most, of our hurt is a reflection or projection of what we see in ourselves. Sometimes the situation is not a projection of ourselves, but in most relationships, we will find that what angers, hurts, or irritates us most about someone else has something to do with us!

For example, when I get upset with Roger's inability to admit that he is wrong, what I'm really frustrated about is that I have a difficult time admitting when I am wrong! When I acknowledge this principle, I see the plank in my own eye and realize my similar weaknesses. This acknowledgment makes it easier to forgive Roger.

We have found that it is more typical to resist looking for the plank in our own eyes or lives, and much easier to complain about or criticize others. But real growth, less judgmentalism, and better relationships take place when we lean into this practical biblical principle.

7. *Forgiveness is not a feeling.* It is a decision! Often, even when you forgive a person, you still feel some degree of pain. You need to realize that forgiveness doesn't mean that you will feel all better immediately. It may take some time before you feel free from the hurt the person has caused you.

Love Means Saying, "I'm Sorry"

In *The Secret of Loving,* Josh McDowell writes, "Forgiveness, when regularly practiced in marriage, leads to increased intimacy because it spawns open communication. If someone loves you despite your faults and accepts you even after you've wronged them, you can't help but respond to that person with an even deeper love" (p. 123).

So many times, I've been so frustrated or angry with Roger, but the action that swiftly melts my heart, quickly changes my mind, and reverses my racing pulse is his acknowledgment that he has hurt me. When he proceeds to share how he has hurt me, then requests forgiveness, I *know* that he has seen my pain and wants to comfort me.

Asking and extending forgiveness have a definitive way of starting a couple down a healing path. We'd encourage you to take that path as often and as swiftly as possible!

■ *Chapter 6* ■

CONFLICT RESOLUTION

In *Fighting for Your Marriage*, the authors claim, "It's not how much you love one another, how good your sex life is, or what problems you have with money that best predicts the future quality of your marriage. . . . The best predictor of marital success is the way you handle conflicts and disagreements" (p. 6).

Conflict is an inevitable, unavoidable reality of life. To have successful relationships, people must resolve rather than ignore conflicts. Unfortunately, many people have very poor systems for resolving conflicts. They may demand, withdraw, withhold, criticize, use power, belittle, attack, or pout. These methods will not achieve a *mutually* satisfactory resolution to conflict. The person relying on such tactics may get what he or she wants, but the relationship will be sabotaged, and the long-term effects are often disastrous. Many relationships have dissolved because couples have repeatedly attempted to use ineffective strategies for dealing with their conflicts and differences. Therefore, *how* we handle conflict will determine the longevity, quality, and health of our relationships.

Roger and I have had conflicts while on vacation, at dinner, over the purchase of gifts, about our finances, sex, parenting, shopping, working, golfing, and church, even while writing this book. We have discovered in the past twenty years that *any* issue has the potential for conflict!

To effectively resolve conflicts, it is important that you use the knowledge and skills covered in the previous chapters of this book, such as good listening techniques, anger control, the rules for effective communication, and understanding your differing needs and personalities. (If you have picked up this book and turned immediately to this chapter because you are in the midst of a conflict you want to resolve, please know that the following system for conflict resolution requires the use of the previously mentioned knowledge and skills.)

Because conflict is one of the main reasons Roger has been counseling couples, families, and individuals for more than fifteen years, he has established a six-step conflict resolution system.

A SIX-STEP CONFLICT RESOLUTION SYSTEM

Step One: Call on God immediately! Either by yourself or with the other person, ask God to help you resolve the pending issue without causing any more damage to your relationship than has already been done. Roger suggests using the following prayer:

Lord, help us to resolve this conflict. Help us not to hurt each other. We know we are in a spiritual battle because the Bible says that we do not fight against flesh and blood, but against the evil forces. We need Your help, Your wisdom, and Your understanding. We are both hurting and are thankful that we can come to You for help. Please help us. We are both imperfect and in need of forgiveness and grace. We both love You and we love each other. Help us to resolve this conflict. In Jesus' name, we pray. Amen.

To pray to God is to admit that you need outside help to resolve your conflict. It brings accountability and humility into the situation, and invites God to intervene.

Step Two: Check the time. In this step, your goal is to agree upon a time and place to talk. Realistically, you may not be able to resolve the conflict *in* or *at* that moment. It is best to decide together *when* to deal with the issue. You should try to find a safe place that is free from distractions for you to talk. Preferably, set the time to talk as soon as possible. Ephesians 4:26–27 is a strong reminder that we should attempt to resolve our conflicts on the same day: "Do not let the sun go down while you are still angry, and do not give the devil a foothold" (NIV). Therefore, whenever possible, schedule it on the day of the conflict. Once you have established the place and time to talk, you are ready for Step Three.

Step Three: Identify the problem. Usually, each person brings different feelings, thoughts, perspectives, and hurts to the situation. Identifying them often requires a significant amount of effort—much more than just giving up or getting angrier. Therefore, during Step Three, each person should share perspectives and feelings about the problem. Stephen Covey's phrase, "Seek first to understand, then to be understood," is a very helpful attitude to embrace during Step Three. Identifying includes listening and understanding. Therefore, Roger encourages the use of the intentional listening skills, as well as the Fourteen Rules for Effective Communication, during this step.

During Step Three, it becomes more evident how each person's ideas, feelings, or desires are conflicting. Try to be as specific as possible to help each person identify the reason for the conflict. During this phase, writing the other person's comments on paper is a way to stay focused while the other person is talking. This can prevent the conversation from spinning out of control.

Let's look at an example of a conflict that revolves around purchasing a car. One person wants a smaller, sporty car, and the other person prefers a larger, more functional sport utility vehicle. Both parties have a fear that they might not get what they want, so each feels the need to persuade the other person. At times they raise their voices or even put each other down. Statements fly, such as, "You are so impractical," and are promptly followed by rebuttals, such as, "Well, you want a big truck." The retorts tend to escalate the conflict and hinder the move to a solution. If both people would share that they *understand* each other's differences in a more objective way, it might look like this:

WIFE: We have different desires. I prefer a car that looks sporty and feels fun. It seems as if you would like a car that is more functional and can carry more people and things. Obviously, we both feel fairly strongly about our desires. Did I understand the issue correctly?

HUSBAND: I agree that we have different desires, but I also think that we differ in what we see as our greatest need at this time. For some reason, you feel a smaller, fun car meets your needs more than a larger vehicle. I want to be able to put sports equipment, boxes, fishing gear, and larger items in our vehicle, and a smaller car doesn't have that capacity. On the other hand, you feel a larger vehicle is not as exciting.

WIFE: So, our problem is that you want a larger vehicle for carrying things, but I really want a smaller car at this time.

In this example, neither party minimized the other person's desires, nor did they get defensive. The goal in this step is to merely identify the conflict. (Note: It is helpful to list all the differing desires and reasons on a sheet of paper, *but only for the purpose of identifying the problem, not trying to solve it*. That step comes later.)

Step Three, if done successfully, serves as a method to be understood. It is of advantage to both when they feel as if their desires or ideas are being heard and understood, even if they are not being met with total agreement.

During this step, we share what each would like to see happen. Admittedly, this is a difficult step because it feels uncomfortable and unsettling to have conflicting desires. At this juncture, both often experience a fear that they won't get what they want. The mutual goal is to move *through* that fear and proceed with the process.

Step Four: Brainstorm possible solutions. There are certain guidelines to observe during this step:

- No idea should be discounted or rejected.
- Resist saying "never" and "always."
- Give each person a chance to share equally or completely, without interruption.
- Listen without criticizing each other.

One of the greatest benefits of the brainstorming step is that it opens us to new ways of thinking. It forces both parties to see that there might be more than one way to solve a problem.

Here is an example of how it can work:

WIFE: Let's brainstorm all of the ways that we can resolve this! We could get the sporty, fun car now, then get the sport utility vehicle in two years. Or we could get a sport utility vehicle now, and a fun, little car in two years.

HUSBAND: Or we could try to find a car that was sporty and fun, but big enough to accommodate more people and equipment.

WIFE: Here's another idea: We could buy two older cars—a smaller, fun car and a sport utility vehicle.

Brainstorming really helps to free each person from the need to hold on to his or her way as the *only* way. It prepares us for the possibility of compromise and moves us to the next step.

Step Five: Find a solution that we will try. During this step, some of the ideas proposed in the brainstorming step will be easy to dismiss because they will not be satisfying to either party. Other solutions will include barriers that will have to be overcome before they can be considered viable solutions. Before a solution can be tried, all the barriers must be discussed.

In the case of the automobile purchase, checking out the financial details, insurance premiums, and so forth will be a prerequisite to assure that there are no additional problems within the solution. If the couple decided on the sports car, they will need to have a plan for hauling larger items at certain times. They might decide to get a roof rack or rent a van a few times a year. All the options should be discussed—in advance—so that there is mutual agreement beforehand.

The fifth step involves a process of compromise, which leads us toward mutual satisfaction. Each person must find some "win" in the solution, but also "give" enough so that the other person will have some level of satisfaction. Stephen Covey calls this a "win-win" situation. In other words, both must feel that we are *getting* something from our agreed upon solution.

To complete the illustration, sometimes your "win" will come at a later date. For example, if the couple decide that the best solution is to get the sport utility vehicle now, the "win" will come for the wife in two years when she gets the sports car. If both parties feel comfortable with their compromise, they have found the "win-win" solution. If either person is going to complain, be critical, resentful, or negative, they are not ready to agree with the solution. They need to keep discussing until they reach a better compromise or discover a different solution, or they must return to the brainstorming step, always keeping in mind that the compromise must be realistic and feasible.

In applying this step to any situation or problem, it is important to understand that every successful relationship will include some sacrifice that is willingly or freely given.

When both parties feel that they have adequately come to a "win-win" solution, and both feel comfortable with decisions they made to resolve any barriers, they have succeeded in sparing their relationship from the danger of poorly resolved or unresolved conflicts.

Step Six: Try the solution and evaluate its effectiveness! In the case of buying a car, this sixth step can be more complicated, and expensive because a car is not returnable! But some decisions can be tried for a week or a month, then both parties can evaluate how the decision worked. If necessary, they can brainstorm, then try new solutions.

Points to Post

A Six-Step Plan to Deal with Conflicts

Step One: Call on God Immediately!
Pray for yourself first: "God, give me the power, the humility, and the control to pray with _____."
Now hold hands (if possible) and pray together:

Lord, help us to resolve this conflict. Help us not to hurt each other. We know we are in a spiritual battle because the Bible says that we do not fight against flesh and blood, but against the evil forces. We need Your help, Your wisdom, and Your understanding. We are both hurting and are thankful that we can come to You for help. Please help us. We are both imperfect and in need of forgiveness and grace. We both love You and we love each other. Help us to resolve this conflict. In Jesus' name, we pray. Amen.

Step Two: Check the Time

Is this an okay time to deal with this conflict? If not, when can we find a time to resolve our problem? Find both a time and a place that are safe for each other and the family.

Step Three: Identify the Problem

(*a*) Practice intentional listening.

(*b*) Obey the Fourteen Rules for Effective Communication.

(*c*) Share perspectives and feelings.

(*d*) Formulate together a statement that identifies the conflict clearly and encompasses both people's feelings and desires.

Step Four: Brainstorm Possible Solutions

No idea is a bad idea. Share several possibilities. Resist using any put-downs or saying that a certain idea won't or can't work. Just come up with possibilities.

Step Five: Find a Solution That We Will Try

Identify barriers to various solutions. Find a win-win solution. Compromise when needed. If you are going to submit and resent, you most likely have not found the right solution. Make a plan. Be specific. Determine the benefits of the plan.

Step Six: Try the Solution and Evaluate Its Effectiveness

Set a time to reevaluate how the solution is working. If the solution is not working, go back to Steps Four and Five.

■ *Chapter 7* ■

FINANCIAL MANAGEMENT

Finances can be a major source of relational tension and friction. The way that our parents managed money, our different personalities, and our expectations and skills in money management are just a few factors that influence our thoughts and patterns regarding money.

Early in our marriage, Roger and I were in ministry positions where we made a limited amount of money. In fact, we lived from paycheck to paycheck. At that time, having a savings or retirement account seemed unachievable from our perspective. We had to be *very* careful with credit cards and often had to squelch our material desires. We were acutely aware that unless we established a budget and followed certain guidelines to assist us in managing our finances, we were prime targets for financial disaster.

MAKE WISE DECISIONS ABOUT
HOW TO SPEND AND SAVE MONEY

The first decision we made was to limit ourselves to a specific amount of personal spending money (aka *allowance*). (Roger spent more of his money eating out. I reserved my allowance for buying clothes!)

The next guideline was to abide by a mutual agreement that neither of us would spend more than fifty dollars without asking permission to do so from the other person. That served as a safety net for our impulsive personalities because both of us were prone to spending more than we could afford. Looking back, we feel that this guideline truly gave us accountability and helped us be cautious with our limited finances. We believe that it literally kept us from spending out of control.

For example, when I went to a store and wanted to buy a sweater that was more than fifty dollars, I knew I had to go home first (or call) and discuss the purchase with Roger. He was required to live by the same guideline. You can't imagine how many times this inconvenient process served its purpose in weeding out our needs from our wants! Though we both found it somewhat restrictive at times, we firmly believe that without such a system we could have very easily gotten into debt.

DEVELOP A BUDGET

Also, early in our marriage, we developed a budget. We wrote down all of our expenses in great detail. Listing our costs for housing, automobile, clothing, insurance, entertainment, and personal needs, we hammered out a workable, realistic budget that we could follow from paycheck to paycheck. We monitored our spending, using large envelopes to hold our out-to-eat money, clothing cash, and individual spending money. Sometimes, we even moved money from one envelope to another, depending upon our desires—unless of course, the money wasn't there! It was never easy, but it proved to be an indispensable system for our financial survival as well as a practical tool for ensuring a healthy relationship.

We want to strongly encourage you to establish a workable, practical budget in order to avoid financial conflicts, which can create additional problems in your relationship. The following budget is a general idea of how you can appropriate your income and expenses. To be completely accurate with this or any budget, you will need to add any areas that are not included, but that are particular to your situation.

This is a monthly budget, so items such as vacations or other bills paid quarterly will need to be broken down into a monthly figure. For example, Christmas or wedding gifts should be divided over twelve months and saved for monthly. In this way you protect yourself from needing to credit-card your way through Christmas, or having to pay interest payments on those gifts for the next six months.

MONTHLY BUDGET

INCOME
Monthly:
His   _____
Hers   _____
Other   _____
_____ _____

TOTAL
INCOME: _____

EXPENSES

Food:		**Savings:**	
Groceries	_____	College	_____
Out to eat	_____	Retirement	_____
Delivered	_____	Emergency	_____

Housing Expenses:		**Tithe/Giving:**	
Mortgage	_____	List each:	_____
(or rent)		_____	_____
Taxes	_____	_____	_____
Repairs	_____		

Utilities:		**Allowance:**	
Electric	_____	His	_____
Water	_____	Hers	_____
Gas	_____	Kids	_____
Phone	_____		
Cable	_____		
Assoc. fee	_____		
Repairs	_____		
Appliances	_____		

Debt:
Loans   _____
Credit card   _____
Other   _____
_____   _____

Insurance:
Medical   _____
Home owners
(or renters)
Automobile   _____
Life   _____

Automobile:
Car 1 pymt.   _____
Car 2 pymt.   _____
Tolls   _____
Gas   _____
Repairs   _____
License & reg.   _____

Clothing:
Dry cleaning   _____
New his   _____
New hers   _____
New kids   _____

Entertainment:
Shows, etc.   _____
Vacations   _____
Health club   _____
Misc.   _____

Gifts:
Birthday / Ann.   _____
Christmas   _____
Misc. holiday   _____

Misc.   _____
Other   _____

Childcare: _____

Beauty:
Haircuts   _____
Misc.   _____

TOTAL
EXPENSES: _____

ENJOY THE FREEDOM OF
BEING DEBT-FREE

It took us a few years, but we eventually made a decision
to eliminate all credit card debt from our lives. The few
times we weren't careful, we discovered that credit card
debt is easy to get into and very difficult to get out of! It

took us until our tenth year of marriage to agree that we would pay all of our credit cards to a zero balance *each period*, and never make a purchase, other than a vehicle or home, that included interest payments. (In other words, what we couldn't pay for with cash by the end of every month, we could not purchase until the cash was in hand!) Once again, this procedure has served as an accountability factor for not overspending. This financial agreement has caused us to save in advance for vacations, so that they are paid for before we leave. It has also forced us to buy furniture (or large items) only when we have the cash.

Another benefit to a monthly zero balance system is that we worry much less and argue very little about money. And because it always saved us from impulsive spending, we still discuss large purchases before making them. And the greatest benefit of not having monthly debt has been the ability to save for our son's education and begin a retirement account.

BLESSINGS ARE IN STORE FOR THE FINANCIALLY WISE COUPLE

We believe that God will financially bless people who are good stewards of their money. As good stewards, we give a percentage of our first earnings to God (tithe), stay away from debt, and have discovered that saving for our future and/or our child's future is wise.

At this point, we feel that it is important for us to discuss the effect of work on your family. Most individuals entering into a marriage relationship are working. We suggest that continual discussions regarding this issue must be held, from the beginning of your relationship throughout all the seasons of your life. Questions similar to the following are great discussion starters:

- How many hours a week do we find it acceptable for us to work?
- How much money do we feel we have to earn to meet our budget and maintain the lifestyle we desire?
- Will both of us work once we have children?
- What effect will that have upon our children?
- If we find that work is taking too much time away from our family, what adjustments are we willing to make?

Though the management of your money will vary with each new job, new home, new child, new purchase, or even unexpected expense, the nonnegotiables should remain:

- Don't spend more money than you make in one month. Live on a budget, and make regular adjustments.
- Pay tithes, taxes, and all bills on time!
- Pay yourself (save for retirement) and save for your children's future in a planned account, even if only a small amount. Good intention is not enough to make this a habit!

We have been fortunate over the past twenty years

- to realize that wise financial management was critical to a healthy relationship.

- to agree upon giving 10 percent (or more) of our earnings back to God, from the first day of our marriage to the present.
- to use whatever methods worked at each juncture of our lives to keep us out of debt.

The result has been that we have not allowed one of the three biggest marital difficulties (sex, money, or poor communication) to weasel its way into our relationship.

Financial management is a necessary skill to master if you desire a successful relationship. A fresh start, a renewed commitment, a visible budget, and perhaps even outside accountability will allow you to make progress and achieve your goals in this area. We encourage you to make it a priority!

■ *Chapter 8* ■

SEXUAL INTIMACY

Sexual intimacy is a very important aspect in marriage, yet like each of the other relationship skills, success in this area doesn't always come naturally. It often takes extra interest, effort, and hard work to develop! Just as you learn about each other's personality differences and needs, you must also learn about your partner's sexual ideas and desires.

COMMUNICATION IS KEY TO SUCCESSFUL SEX!

Good communication can go a long way in enhancing a couple's lovemaking. That communication must be consistent with love: tender, patient, kind, and understanding. If the sexual conversation is characterized by demanding, harsh tones or words, you need to make adjustments in that area. Talking to each other about what does or doesn't please you, how often you would like to be sexually intimate, and what are appropriate "mood setters" and what may be "mood hurters" will lead to better sexual intimacy.

KEEP ROMANCE AND CREATIVITY IN YOUR MARRIAGE

Keep your sexual relationship fun and exciting. Being passionate, romantic, and creative will give you pleasure and help your marriage stay vibrant. Clifford and Joyce Penner have written a wonderful little book entitled *52 Ways to Have Fun, Fantastic Sex*. They offer concrete ideas such as surprising your mate at a different time of the day and experimenting with new positions to enhance your love life. We recommend this book, as well as other books that they have written, to assist you in maintaining excitement in your sexual relationship. They note one important caution that we pass on to you as well. Never go against your partner's will or choice in the area of sexual creativity.

When Roger conducts his premarital instructions, he asks the couples to complete a sexual inventory. The couples are able to learn much about each other's fears, hopes, and desires by honestly answering the questions in private, then sharing their answers with each other in the presence of a counselor. Here are some questions Roger asks the couples to discuss:

- How many times do you expect to have sexual intercourse in a week?
- Do you have any fears regarding your sex life? If so, what are they?
- To enjoy the best sex, do you believe that you need to reach orgasm together?

- How would you feel about talking or being silent during lovemaking?
- Are there any sexual activities you would rather not practice?
- Can you share any idea that would give you a satisfying sex life?
- Will you go for counseling if you have difficulty achieving sexual satisfaction? If so, how long will you wait before seeing a counselor?
- How important is gentle caressing to your sexual intercourse?
- Is the best lovemaking position for the man to be on top of the woman? How do you feel about trying different positions?
- Is it acceptable to satisfy each other without sexual intercourse?
- How will you feel if either of you fails to reach a climax? Will it mean that you have failed in the sexual area?
- What happens if one of you doesn't want to have sex?
- If you are going to use birth control, what method or methods will you use? Whose responsibility will birth control be?
- Will it be better for you to make love with the lights off, low, or in daylight?
- How would you feel about getting excited sexually and then not having sexual intercourse? Do you think it is healthy or unhealthy to do so?
- Are there any areas related to sex that bother or confuse you?
- Is there anything in your past that might affect your sex life? Explain.

(You and your spouse might want to answer these questions now, or later, if you choose to discuss the questions at the end of the book. The goal of these questions is to create a healthy, open discussion with your spouse about your sex life.)

Once you begin communicating with your spouse, you may discover a mutual desire for practical information on enhancing your sexual relationship. There are a number of resources on the mechanics, methods, and mysteries of sexual pleasure written by Christian professionals, such as Norman Wright, and Clifford and Joyce Penner.

Believing that the skill of sexual intimacy is learned, Roger gives each of his premarital couples a wedding gift of Dr. Douglas Rosenau's book, *A Celebration of Sex*. Within its pages are topics such as creative romance, playfulness, enhancing pleasure, and resolving problems. Just as there are problems that arise between a couple in the area of communication or finances, there are many problems that can occur between a couple in the area of sexuality.

DEALING WITH SEXUAL DYSFUNCTION

Unfortunately, in the society in which we live, there is an unhealthy focus on sexuality. Extramarital affairs glamorized in the media, pornography on the Internet, and sexual abuse are only a few of the reasons that so many of us struggle with some form of sexual dysfunction. Ultimately, these outside influences hinder normal sexual satisfaction.

We believe that it is very difficult to deal with dysfunctional sexuality on your own. Recovering from sexual dysfunction is rarely a self-help project. If you are facing one of the challenges listed in this section, we urge you to find a support group or counselor you trust and work through your particular problem.

Pornography

If you have been exposed to pornography, which obviously is a focus on the sex act as opposed to the love relationship, then you have to make an intentional effort to move away from the temptation of pornography. If you have fallen prey to pornography, you may struggle with viewing the other person as an object for sex rather than a person to love. You must tell yourself to focus on behavior that manifests love. Roger warns people who have viewed a great deal of pornography of its negative effects. He encourages couples who are dealing with this problem to show more affection and spend more time on demonstrating love for the partner. This helps them to focus more on the love in the relationship and less on the sex act. We strongly suggest that you become accountable to one or more persons regarding this area in your life.

Promiscuity and Sexual Abuse

Your sexual past can adversely affect your marriage. Unhealthy sexual experiences and/or the lack of solid, moral sex education can cause guilt, pain, and inhibitions, resulting in sexual dysfunction within marriage. When there has been sexual promiscuity or sexual abuse, or when an individual has grown up in a home where sex was taught or displayed in unhealthy ways, counseling is usually needed.

I have had to deal with a past that included sexual immorality. My emotional struggles in this area have had a negative effect on my sexual intimacy with Roger. I have had to continually work to improve this area of my life. For many years, I have been a part of support groups where sharing my past has helped me in my recovery process. In addition, reading Neil Anderson's *Freedom from Bondage* prompted me to pray through the *7 Steps to Freedom* with a pastoral counselor and friend, which was very helpful. Most important, Roger and I have been very open and honest to communicate about how my past affects our current sex life. Though it hasn't been easy for him, Roger's patience and understanding have been extremely important factors in my continued healing.

Performance Anxiety

Another hindrance to sexual satisfaction, especially common among men, is called performance anxiety. It refers to the anxiety a person feels regarding the ability to perform sexually. This anxiousness or fear has different intensities. The higher the intensity, the more negative its effect upon a couple's sexual relationship. Instead of focusing on the relationship, the person becomes focused on the performance and is hindered from experiencing sexual satisfaction.

In *Restoring the Pleasure*, Clifford and Joyce Penner suggest that a man express his concerns to his wife as soon as he begins feeling anxious:

Many men are concerned that telling their wives about their worries will only make both of them feel more discouraged and frustrated. There is a tendency to want to ignore the thoughts and feelings with the hope that they will go away and will not negatively affect the response. However, if the anxiety is not expressed (switched from the right brain to the left brain), it will become more overpowering. . . . Thus, interrupting the anxiety by expressing it is absolutely necessary. (P. 243)

If this is an ongoing problem in your relationship, seeking outside help would be wise.

Sexual Addiction

Sexual addiction is prevalent in our society. The allure of the illicit has destroyed many relationships. It takes a very strong stand to overcome the sexual temptations so prominent in the mainstream media. The only proper response to illicit sexual temptation is for each person to close the door to *any* sexual experience outside the marriage relationship.

It is critical for people tempted in this area to get into a support group or counseling situation that will help them be accountable to sexual purity. Searching to understand the root of this intense desire is as important as taking the responsibility to abstain from illicit sexual behavior.

Often, sexual addiction has deep roots, and sex has been used to numb the pain. Growing up in homes where there have been less than adequate amounts of encouragement, support, and nurture will create a void or cause deep pain. Many have attempted to fill this void or numb this pain through inappropriate sexual behavior. Relying on sexual experiences over a long period of time as a way to deal with the void or pain begins to develop a pattern and often turns into an addiction. Most people can't imagine themselves being addicted to sex, but if they honestly analyzed their behavior, they would find out that they are.

The Penners devote an entire chapter to "controlling sexual addictions" in *Restoring the Pleasure,* defining the dysfunction, describing the patterns and cycles, and even providing a key list of questions that can help determine if you are sexually addicted. If you have any concerns, reservations, or red flags about this area, we strongly urge you to take the necessary steps to seek outside help for the sake of your marriage.

Don't Be Afraid or Embarrassed to Get Help

Time after time, Roger has met with people who have tried to stop certain inappropriate sexual behavior by themselves, but they couldn't. Failed attempts at individual preventive measures have often driven them into more illicit sexual relationships, pornography, or other unhealthy sexual exploitations. Meeting with a professional Christian counselor and/or getting into a support group where you can deal honestly with dysfunctional or unhealthy sexuality is essential in dealing with this issue. Far too many people are attempting to deal with these problems on their own, and for the most part, their methods are ineffective. To those who might be in this situation, we say, *Don't be afraid or embarrassed to get help!!!*

This book is not designed to provide in-depth help to resolve major sexual dysfunction or dissatisfaction. We recommend Dr. Douglas Rosenau's *A Celebration of Sex*. He does a very thorough job of helping couples understand the positive and painful dimensions of sex. The book discusses, in detail, lovemaking as well as dysfunction in the sexual arena.

The excellent book *Broken Promises: Healing and Preventing Affairs in Christian Marriages* by Henry Virkler explains ways to avoid affairs and what to do if there is or has been unfaithfulness in the relationship.

ANOTHER GREAT RESOURCE ON SEX

Perhaps the greatest resource on sexuality is the Bible. In the Song of Songs, sexual intimacy is described as romantic and exciting. In the book of Proverbs, chapter 5, sexual satisfaction is portrayed as passionate. The New Testament discusses sex from a moral perspective. In 1 Corinthians and Ephesians, sex is depicted as the privileged union between married persons.

God intended for married couples to experience sexual pleasure during their lifetime together! We encourage you to develop your sexual intimacy and to enjoy the gift that God has given you.

■ *Chapter 9* ■

PARENTING

The primary purpose of this book is to encourage spouses to have a successful relationship with each other. But since your relationship possibly includes children, we provide a section on *positive parenting skills*.

Roger and I have been parents almost as long as we've been married, and we can honestly say that we consider our only son, Jake, to be one of the greatest blessings of our marriage! Jake entered into our relationship only ten days after our first anniversary, and because we became a threesome so early in our marriage, we learned that the very same knowledge and skills that applied to our relationship were also effective in parenting.

As important as it was to understand each other's personality types, it was just as helpful to understand Jake's basic personality type and traits. We realized early in his life that he is primarily a sanguine child who lives for and loves to have *fun*! We *love* his personality! He negotiates extremely well, enjoys every type of sport, and makes one person or a whole room laugh with his words, gestures, and funny expressions. Roger and I often comment that we feel very fortunate that he is more a blend of our strengths than our weaknesses. As parents, we recognized and understood his strengths *and* weaknesses. This information has been helpful in teaching, disciplining, and motivating him, especially throughout his elementary and secondary education.

We raised Jake during the 1980s, under the tutelage of the child-rearing guru of our parenting days, Dr. James Dobson. From his books we gleaned a few great skills:

- Be in mutual agreement as parents regarding the discipline of your child—and be consistent.
- Don't hit or spank with your hand, but when appropriate, use a wooden spoon to administer discipline. And don't discipline out of *your anger,* but because of *your child's disobedience.*
- Be firm, but loving. Speak lovingly, touch lovingly, and never withhold love. Work hard at finding the right balance between love and discipline.

TEN POSITIVE PARENTING SKILLS

Through the past nineteen years of parenting, Roger and I have developed a few of our own *positive parenting skills* that have helped us raise a child who loves God and his parents in a society that doesn't often promote that same agenda!

Positive Parenting Skill #1: Model your faith. Teach your children to have a loving relationship with God!

From the time that Jacob was old enough to eat, we began to teach him to say prayers, thanking God for his food and whatever else came to his mind. Children have a way of praying openly and sincerely about the things that are important to them. And true to Jake's personality and needs, his prayers before a meal or at bedtime were, "Help us to have a good day," or "Thank You for a fun day!"

Early in the parenting process, we modeled to Jacob that we have an appointed time with God every day that we call our quiet time. Both Roger and I use *My Partner Prayer Notebook* as the place where we journal and write out our conversations with the Lord on a daily basis. In fact, one of the things that I taught Jacob as a child was that when I was praying or having my quiet time, I should not be interrupted unless it was something important. He was always very considerate of my hour appointments. But when he had reached a point of too much silence, he would run over to the stove alarm (which I would set to ring in one hour from the time that I started my appointment) and see how many minutes were left for me to pray. He would then know how long it would be before I was free to talk or play or do something else. He'd often yell to me, "Twenty more minutes!" signaling that my time was almost up!

As Jacob grew older, Roger and I would go to his room each night and pray with him over general and very specific requests. If he was needing help with an attitude, we would teach him to talk to the Lord about it, asking for help and forgiveness when necessary. If he was looking for a very specific answer to a request, we would help him to formulate his request, based on biblical principles. But as we have learned from our own prayer lives, the Bible encourages us to ask God and ask about everything! James 4:2–3 declares, "You do not have, because you do not ask God. When you ask, you do not receive, because you ask with wrong motives" (NIV), and Philippians 4:6 urges, "Pray about everything" (NLT). Because Roger and I are committed to talking to God on a daily basis about all of our concerns, we have encouraged Jacob to do the same.

Using any methods that a parent can to encourage kids to pray is our motto! Every child is motivated and will respond to things differently; therefore, you may need to try various methods to teach children to pray.

As a firm believer that prayer changes lives, I have even held a twenty-minute weekly prayer meeting in my home for the last two years with some of Jake's high school friends. Why? Because praying out loud with someone who loves to pray is one method to increase students' interest in a spiritual discipline that might otherwise seem boring to them!

The goal in our personal prayer lives, and in teaching Jake how to pray, has not been to become better people or better Christians. We pray, and have taught Jake to pray to the Lord, our God, in order to develop a loving, intimate relationship with Him. We believe strongly that the benefits of an active, transparent, conversational prayer life are innumerable. But the most important one is that each person improves his or her relationships with God and others when having daily conversations with Him. We have also found that it is not wise to pressure your kids to do something that you find too difficult to do! Having children is sometimes one of the most compelling reasons to develop your prayer life!

Positive Parenting Skill #2: Pray regularly, and fast for your children.

By the time Jacob entered high school and started driving, my prayer list for him had grown from one to four pages! I have prayed for his grades, his classes, his teachers, and each of his friends by name. Just to give you an idea of how many things a teenager needs prayer for, I've included the following pages of my prayer list for Jake:

A Prayer List for Jacob:
Physical growth and health:

- Height (to increase to 5′10″)
- Weight (to increase to 140#)
- Seven habits of an eighteen-year-old—to fill in the chart
- Track—success this year
- Golf—enjoy with us and friends
- Contacts or glasses?
- Eat right and sleep enough
- To grow daily more handsome and strong

Mental growth:

- Make principal's list at school (yea! 3.75)
- A's in senior year

- To find Youth in Government to be interesting
- To have fun in Sacramento
- Enjoy work, get good hours

Spiritual growth:

- Attend big church regularly, and/or high school group and/or Rock
- Read and pray daily
- Attend Worldview Camp
- Connect with You and a staff person on ski trip
- Go to Mexicali over spring break?
- Share his faith with his friends

Emotional growth:

- Grow in responsibility
- Avoid/hate procrastination
- Develop: integrity, godliness, neatness, discipline, honesty, wisdom, strength, perseverance, determination, holiness, kindness, purity
- To be safe on Prom Night and Grad Night

In addition:

- Twenty-five of Jake's friends by name
- A truck—help us to buy the one for his eighteenth birthday at a price that is reasonable. Please show us where and when; and open his heart to increased responsibility.
- His future wife: To be loved and protected by You and her parents. To be pure and funny and to love You, Lord. For her parents to be fun! (I figure that we'll have to spend time together!)
- His major in college (?)

A fasting strategy for Jacob. In May 1995, I read Bill Bright's *The Coming Revival,* which taught me much about the power of fasting and prayer. It was an exciting book that compelled me to embark on a forty-day partial fast for the purpose of growing closer to God and listening to Him more intently. In addition, I asked Him to show me what I could do to make a difference in my country for Him. The results were phenomenal, and after seeing how many things had changed or turned around as a result of that forty-day partial fast (June–July 1995), I felt led to fast for my son one day (until dinner) each week during the rest of his high school years.

At the end of Jake's junior year, it seemed as if his finals were going to be tougher than ever! That worried me because I was under the impression that it couldn't get any harder! So I told Jake, "Okay, kiddo. I'm going to go out on a limb for you here! I'm going to fast all three days of your finals this year: Monday, Tuesday, and Wednesday."

His short reply was, "Good. I need it."

That didn't particularly encourage me, but it did motivate me! On Monday afternoon when he came home from the first round of finals, I said, "How'd you do?"

His short reply was, "Keep fasting!"

On Wednesday, school was over for the summer, and the kids were all going out to celebrate.

I had been fasting since Sunday, so all I wanted to think about was food and that my job was done. But a nagging thought lingered: *You said that you would fast all three days for Jacob. Just finish out the day, and your job will be done tomorrow!*

I went to bed hungry, but Roger and I woke up at 1:00 A.M. to a dark figure standing at our door frame. It was our son, who had only one thing to say, "I just want you to know that I was one of the few people who didn't drink tonight, and it wasn't *fun!*"

He wasn't happy, and he obviously felt as if he had been left out of a good time. But because we had previously discussed the subject of drinking (from every angle, but primarily his genetic makeup, which included my own alcoholism) and had asked him not to drink, Jacob had toed the line, kept his promise, bitten the bullet, and honored us in spite of the pressure, rejection, and temptation.

My very first thought was, *No, you weren't just fasting for his finals. You were also fasting for this very night when he would be challenged and tested. He made it through the night. And it wasn't fun, and it wasn't easy. And who knows how important your fast was in helping him overcome the odds against him?* Hot tears rolled down my cheeks as he headed back to his bedroom.

Roger and I have been diligent to fast weekly and pray daily for our precious son. And I imagine that we will continue to do so until the day we die!

Positive Parenting Skill #3: Treat your children with respect. Talk to them in the same tone of voice in which you would like to be spoken.

In 1984, I made a personal decision to spend one hour a day in prayer. Shortly after I had made a commitment, many things began to change in our household. Not only was I becoming more organized (a better steward of my time), but I was becoming more receptive to making the changes in my life that God required.

One of the most evident bad habits that I exhibited in the privacy of my home was yelling and screaming at Jacob. Though I never exhibited this out-of-control behavior in public, my lack of self-control in private became an area of my life that I wanted to change, especially because of the negative, long-lasting impact it was bound to have on Jake. (I was aware of the resentment that yelling at your child can build, but I hadn't been willing to change my behavior until Jake was four years old.)

I made a promise to God and Jake that I would yell at him only "up to a certain volume level." That was fine with Jake and worked great for several months, even years. One day, however, when Jake was about eleven years old, we were getting ready to go to a Little League game, and Jake couldn't find his glove. (This trait of losing everything is typical of sanguine personalities, and to this day, we *regularly* search for Jake's wallet and keys!) I was irritable and said, "Look, we will be late if we don't leave right now. You'll have to use Daddy's good black leather glove. But if you lose Daddy's glove, you are going to get the biggest lickin' of your lifetime!"

Jake pitched a great game, and we headed home. As we pulled into the driveway, it dawned on me that I hadn't seen Jake come home with a glove. Indeed, Jake had left his daddy's glove at the field! Two houses to the left and two houses to the right heard me scream at the top of my lungs, "Jacob . . . Anthony . . . Tirabassiiiiii!" As I repeated the threat of the biggest lickin' in his life on our way back to the ballpark, little Jake clasped his hands together and began praying, "Dear Jesus . . ." Before he could finish, this out-of-control mom replied, "Don't even pray!"

Fortunately, as Jake ran up to the coach to explain his dilemma, the coach's smiling face told us that the glove had been found. When the coach held it up for Jake to take home, Jake replied, "Thank You, Jesus!"

On the way home, I continued to berate him for losing the glove, to which he replied, "Mom, we found the glove. What's the problem?"

Not wanting to admit my lack of self-control, I said, "Well, maybe it's the wrong time of the month."

Jake said, "Oh. You mean that MBM."

"What's an MBM?" I asked.

"Mom's Bad Mood!" he replied. "Can little boys get that? I've been getting into trouble lately, losing things . . ."

"No, Jake, it's called PMS and little boys can't get that!" I did an immediate health lesson, then proceeded to humbly ask his forgiveness, which he gave me, and that was the end of the episode. Or so I thought.

Several days later, Jake's calm, jovial fifth-grade teacher at his Christian school was having a stressful day. As she stood on a chair putting up letters on the bulletin board, the class got too rowdy, and she turned around and firmly stated, "Hey, knock it off!" The class quickly calmed down because she rarely lost her temper.

Jake raised his hand. "Mrs. Brosius," he asked, "do you think you could have PMS?"

Relating the dynamics of this story to me at 3:00 P.M. when I came to pick up Jacob, she told me how she had almost fallen off the chair with laughter! She immediately realized that half of the class understood what PMS was and half didn't. So after a short explanation, she released them all for recess—and proceeded to tell every teacher and even the principal what Jacob had said in class. By the time I had arrived to pick Jake up after school, she was still laughing about "the best line she had heard in twenty years of teaching!"

Roger and I have had to make a conscious effort to control our tempers with our son, and we have remained accountable to each other when we have failed. At every stage of his development, we have struggled with the balance of being firm, yet loving in our communication with him.

But I would add a personal note here. I have told this story at my workshops for many years, and there is rarely a dry eye in the room when I have finished—not because it is such a funny story, but because it is very convicting. If you are a parent who yells and screams at your children, you very well might have grown up in a home where you were yelled and screamed at. But if you think very long or hard about how that made you feel, you probably remember those times with resentment, pain, hurt, anger, or even hatred toward the people who spoke to you or treated you harshly, perhaps even unfairly. Only as adults do we seem to really understand that the angry, out-of-control person has often overreacted or lost control of emotions.

When I came to the honest conclusion that my anger with Jake had more to do with me than him, I was able to stop treating him in a demeaning, hurtful way. I have had to force myself, many times, to be gentle or kind, a better listener, more understanding of his personality, and more trustful of his character. I really encourage you to do the same with your children. Perhaps you will have to honestly examine yourself, make some changes, become accountable, even get professional help. But I assure you, the effort that you make to eliminate yelling from your behavior, at home or away from home, will not be wasted.

I am living proof that a yelling, screaming mom can change a bad habit. And the greatest blessing is the fun, loving relationship that I had with my child throughout each stage of his development!

Positive Parenting Skill #4: Teach your children to tithe.

As a couple, we have always practiced the biblical principle of tithing as found in Malachi 3:10, "'Bring the whole tithe into the storehouse, that there may be food in my house. Test me in this,' says the LORD Almighty, 'and see if I will not throw open the floodgates of heaven and pour out so much blessing that you will not have room enough for it'" (NIV).

From the time that Jacob was a little boy, we taught him to give back to the Lord a tenth of the money he received from his allowance and work. One particular experience stands out as an illustration of the blessing we received by following this principle.

Because we worked for a church, we often held Sunday evening student worship services. Only one of the staff couples had a toddler. Since all of us were going to be in the large youth group room, we offered Jacob as a playmate for the toddler, thinking that he could keep her busy in the back of the room during the service. He did a great job of entertaining her, and the young parents were so pleased that they offered to give Jacob a five-dollar bill. We tried to discourage them because they were very young and didn't seem to have a lot of extra cash to spend. In addition, we thought that Jake should offer his time to them free of charge. But they insisted on giving Jake the money!

Before we knew it, Jake put the whole five dollars in the offering plate! I exclaimed, "Jake, that is really great of you, but you don't have to put the whole amount in the offering plate." He still wanted to do it. So I replied, "Now, just watch and see what the Lord is going to do! Perhaps He will multiply it tenfold!"

This is a true story, mind you! The very next day, Jake received a fifty-dollar check in the mail for his eighth birthday from one set of his grandparents! Upon opening the envelope, he yelled from his bedroom, "And it all came in one check!" (Just an editorial note: He didn't receive that gracious amount of money from his grandparents again until his graduation day, almost ten years later!)

Positive Parenting Skill #5: Whenever possible, attend a church that has an excellent children's and/or youth department.

In our early days of marriage and ministry in Cleveland, Ohio, we were fortunate to have board members and friends who had children in junior high and high school.

They showed those of us who had small children how to love and nurture teenagers.

One family did something that truly impacted our way of doing things when our son became a teenager. They had attended a certain church when their children were in elementary school. But when their children hit the teen years, they were adamant about attending a church that focused on teenagers. They realized at that juncture that their particular church did not have a hired youth pastor, nor did it have a fun, active, healthy, growing youth department. It was a small church without an emphasis on youth ministry.

They made a very selfless decision. Even though *they* loved the church, they moved their family to another local church that provided a balance of fun, excitement, activities, and spiritual growth where their kids could learn to love God, serve God, and have positive relationships with many other Christian teenagers.

Both sons were very active in the music and youth ministries of the church. Both attended Christian colleges. And both parents would tell you, to this day, that they sacrificed their "favorite style of music or worship," even listening to their favorite pastor, for the sake of keeping their kids actively involved in a church!

When we faced the same stage, we had no option but to attend a church that catered to our son's spiritual growth. Those churches always had an excellent youth staff and trained volunteers, and provided a place for students both to grow in the Lord and to bring their seeker friends.

As a result, our son has been actively involved in his high school group, has been a part of a small group experience since junior high, and has occasionally volunteered with the younger kids on trips or programs. Some of Jacob's greatest friends are the volunteers and staff who have been his youth leaders in the past. (I can think of at least five of them who *regularly* call our home to ask Jake to play basketball or roller hockey, ride mountain bikes, or go snowboarding or waterskiing. They have become his friends as well as mentors and role models. And what better friends, role models, or examples would you want your kids to hang out with, learn from, and be led by?)

Positive Parenting Skill #6: Say or do the things that you want your children to say or do.

Because Roger and I, but especially I, lived a life of alcohol, drugs, and sexual immorality before becoming Christians, we have been very careful and discerning about what we watch, what we do, and where we go. We take our responsibility to model our values very seriously.

For the first twelve years of our married life we were involved in youth ministry. As role models and leaders to so many teenagers and college-age students, we felt responsible, if not "called," to live by the principle that the best way to teach abstinence, purity, or integrity is to live by the same rules that we want our students to live by. (In other words, we have followed the "Do as I do" philosophy rather than the "Do what I say, not what I do" philosophy.)

When we became parents, we soon realized that we had just been promoted to role models twenty-four hours a day, seven days a week. We purposed to watch television or see movies that were more family oriented. We stocked the refrigerator with plenty of sodas, but no alcohol. And we concentrated on using phrases and clichés that were clean and fun and harmless. We also made it our goal to encourage honesty and truthfulness in the smallest situations in order to develop those virtues as habits.

Guess what? Recently, a schoolmate of Jake's told my husband, "My goal is to hear Jake swear before he graduates this year." (We're praying for that boy!) Other kids have unsuccessfully tried to get Jake to drink.

And just in the last month of his senior year of high school, he got a progress report. The drafting teacher had given Jake a D. Jake had been very sick, causing him to miss a week of school, but he had assured me that he was all caught up on his schoolwork. I called the drafting teacher on the same day that I received the mail, but before I had a chance to talk to Jake. I told the teacher, "Jake told me that he had a 94 percent in your class, and your mark on his report card certainly says otherwise."

Overcome with the emotion of a parent receiving bad news about her child's grades, I only wanted to express my confidence in Jake, even though the "official report" showed the opposite. I said, "I have never known Jacob to lie to me. Would you be willing to check your grade book and see if your progress report could have been filled out incorrectly?" I think the teacher was taken aback by my remark, and agreed that Jacob was a very fine student, and the report could be wrong. Because he was in the main office, he told me that he would have to go back to his classroom, find the grade book, and call me back.

Within the hour he called me back to say that Jacob, indeed, had a 94 percent in the class. He further explained that progress reports had to be turned in during the week of Jacob's illness; therefore, the report wasn't accurate! I was, at that moment, and have been regularly, impressed with my son's character and integrity.

Roger and I believe that though the temptations and pressures in the life of a teenager are great, there is no stronger or more lasting influence in a child's life than his parents' actions, words, and choices. We have missed some critically acclaimed movies and funny television shows, and we have not been invited to certain parties, but we wouldn't change how we have lived our lives in front of our son, nor could we be more proud of the young man we have raised!

Positive Parenting Skill #7: Apologize to your children when it is appropriate. Ask them for forgiveness.

Jake graduated from high school in June of 1997. It was an exciting day for the three T's, but Jake was particularly excited about the shower of gifts that he received from friends and family! I had a request: *No checks get cashed until thank-you notes are written.* That rule was okay with Jake, but it was obvious that the checks were going to stack up rather than get swiftly cashed.

Soon, I felt I had to find a different way to motivate Jake, at least so the bank statements of those generous folks could get balanced in the coming year! So I asked Jake if he would write them within the week. He agreed!

I then proceeded to take his checks to the bank and deposit them into his personal checking account. Somehow, we (or should I say, "I"?) lost track of whose checks got deposited in which of the two deposits that were made.

Somehow, in the process, it appeared as if Jake had misplaced two checks. Roger, Jake, and I spent no less than ninety minutes unraveling every corner of his room, going through his drawers, and rummaging through the garbage, but we could not find the checks. In addition to that tedious procedure, I walked in and out of his bedroom, and up and down the stairway, making comments about too many checks, not writing the thank-you notes in time, and other statements that could have been translated to mean, "I told you this might happen." I recall the word *procrastination* got thrown out that night as well.

Now, no teenager wants to tell someone special that he misplaced the check that he had received as a gift. But the last people he would want to break that kind of bad news to would be his grandparents, especially since his parents had lost a check from them the previous year! Guess what? One of the missing checks was from Jake's grandparents!

Rog and Jake finally came up with a temporary solution. Jake would write thank-you notes to the two families whose checks had been misplaced, and we would continue to hope that the checks would turn up. I thought that was a *bad* idea, but Roger and Jake overruled me.

Then the inevitable occurred. Roger's dad called to let us know that he had received Jake's nice thank-you note. Roger bravely proceeded with the entire explanation that we had misplaced the check, gone through all the garbage, and looked everywhere for it. Roger's dad said, "Well, that's strange, because I just got my bank statement back and the check we wrote to Jacob has been cashed!" So, it never had been lost! In fact, it had been deposited with all of the other checks, but not accounted for!

We laughingly told Jake, but he didn't think it was all that funny. Two days later, he said to me, "Hey, did you ever apologize to me for blaming me for losing a check that I never lost?" (We always ask him to apologize when he is wrong.)

I said, "Oh my gosh, Jake. No. I am so sorry." I hugged him, laughed with him, and hugged him again. Then he said the most natural thing for Jake to say, "You don't need to apologize. Just get me a new wakeboard!" I was no longer laughing.

Positive Parenting Skill #8: Don't say no unless you have to!

For Jacob's thirteenth birthday, he talked Roger into getting him a small dirt bike (off-road motorcycle). I never thought it was a great idea, but when it comes to "guy things," it is always two against one around here.

He got his little yellow dirt bike, but I was never that excited about him riding it or even revving it up in the neighborhood. One Sunday afternoon, he was invited to a friend's house, and the dad was going to pick Jacob up in fifteen minutes. Jake had put on long pants and a nice shirt, but had fifteen minutes to spare! All he could think about was going outside to rev up his dirt bike and give it a spin around the cul-de-sac. I thought that was a bad idea for a number of reasons. I was certain that he would get dirty, which, in turn, would call for a change of clothes and cause him to be late for the dad who was picking him up. In addition, I presumed the neighbors would disapprove of the loud noise I thought the dirt bike would make. So after repeated "beggings," I remained firm with my no.

He was disappointed and went outside just to look at the bike. Roger had observed the whole situation, but didn't get involved until Jacob had retreated. He has always given his parenting advice to me with the goal of enhancing my relationship with Jacob. Therefore, when he sees something that could hurt my relationship with him, although he doesn't bring it up in front of Jacob, he tries to show me how to make our relationship more of a "win-win." He simply said, "As a general rule of thumb, I try not to say no to Jacob unless I have to. There are going to be many things through Jake's adolescence that we will have to say no about, Becky. If this is not a big deal, I wouldn't say no simply because it is inconvenient."

It took me only a few minutes to rethink the situation. And using Roger's "rule of thumb" as a guideline prompted me to call outside to Jake, "Hey, Jake. I've changed my mind. You probably have enough time to rev up that motorcycle if you still want to do that." He did—with plenty of time to spare!

Positive Parenting Skill #9: Be loving toward your spouse in front of your children.

Show your kids that you love each other. Be affectionate and affirming in front of them. Say the words, "I love you," often to your spouse *and* your kids. If you and your spouse have a disagreement in front of the children, use the communication skills previously discussed, showing them that you can communicate without wounding each other. While you are in front of them, when appropriate, ask and give forgiveness to each other. Otherwise, reserve your more heated conflicts for times and places where you have more time and privacy to adequately resolve your differences.

Positive Parenting Skill #10: As your children get older, discuss and evaluate curfews, discipline measures, expectations, and finances (gifts, work, chores, allowance, etc.).

Because these things regularly need revision, schedule a family meeting that results in mutual agreement.

By the time Jake entered high school, it seemed as if a chart was the best way to keep him accountable to the chores and responsibilities that we had mutually agreed upon for him to do on a daily basis. The following chart is one that I devised for Jake once he began driving and working! It served as a guide, a reminder, and an accountability tool. It was not used 100 percent of the time, but I designed this chart with the hope of helping my high school son develop disciplines and habits that would positively affect his future!

THE SEVEN HABITS OF A HIGHLY SUCCESSFUL STUDENT

Day or Date	Clean Room	School Manage-ment	Clean Car	Clean Bath-room	Spiritual Growth	Sleep and Eat Enough	Banking

SHARING THE PARENTING

Ironically, Roger and I would tell you that our greatest joy and perhaps our greatest corporate success has been our only child, Jacob. I say "ironically," because we seriously considered *never* having children. We told our pastor in premarital counseling sessions that we might not ever have children. But just three months after we were married, Roger told me that he sensed that God was prompting us to have a child! I was taken off guard, not even thinking I would have to consider having children for years to come, if at all! We spent the next few days discussing and praying about God's will for our lives in this area. We decided to eliminate our birth control measures and . . . guess what? About one week later, I got pregnant, and only ten days after our first anniversary, we were a family of three!

Perhaps life changes more for the mother of a child, but I never felt that I was alone in the parenting of our son. From February 8, 1979, until the present, Roger and I have been equally responsible for Jake's care: emotionally, physically, and spiritually. When Jake was a preschooler, I didn't go into an office. I worked out of my home or as a volunteer. When Jake entered elementary school, I arranged a part-time schedule to work around the daily school schedule and calendar. In summers, I decreased my office hours and worked at home or evenings when Rog was available to be home. And when I began to travel, Roger resigned his full-time job in order to become the full-time at-home parent of a teenager (mainly after school, evenings, and weekends). Our goal was to daily have a parent at home during the hours when our son was home, and we maintained that approach to parenting until our son left for college.

Our greatest satisfaction is that we don't have personal regrets for spending less time working and more time parenting! Though our retirement and bank accounts may be smaller than they could be, our precious memory accounts of Jake are full!

What has been our hope in parenting Jacob? We have desired to raise a child who would grow in favor with God and humankind! And judging by his good reputation and the truly wonderful friends he has gained through the years, as well as the personal pride, joy, pleasure, and respect that we have for our son, we believe that following these parenting skills has led us to success.

Of course, parenting is never finished, and we're not out of the woods yet. Therefore, we will continue to employ the tools of listening with intent and use self-control and conflict management as lifelong skills in our relationship with Jacob, as well as with each other. We have found that whenever we can't be with him in person, we can be there in prayer! In addition, we will more than likely fast regularly for our son until the day we die because we know that he is on the journey of life that holds inevitable twists and turns, adventures, trials, and joy!

PART 3

THE DECISIONS NECESSARY FOR SUCCESSFUL RELATIONSHIPS

■ *Chapter 10* ■

Stay Connected to God

Through very painful experiences, both Roger and I learned the high cost of not staying connected to God.

OUR STORIES

Roger is convinced that not staying connected to God cost him his first marriage. He believes that the lack of a spiritual dimension in his life hindered his ability to love, be sacrificial, or be sensitive to God or others. Roger became a Christian at age twenty-six, after his divorce. In March of 1973, he made a decision to stay connected to God for the rest of his life.

Not staying connected to God almost cost me my life!

In the early 1970s, I moved from Cleveland to California and began living a loose, immoral lifestyle. By 1976, I "hit bottom" with alcohol, drugs, and immorality. Though

I was trying to fill my life with a variety of spirits, there was one obvious void. I was not connected to God in any way, even though I had been raised with the midwestern, churchgoing mentality of the 1950s and 1960s. Both my out-of-control lifestyle and my California live-in relationship almost ended tragically when I considered suicide on August 26, 1976. Instead of taking my life, I drove to a church where a janitor led me to Christ in a prayer. On that day, I decided to connect with and stay connected to God for the rest of my life.

Our stories are not unique. Many people attribute their failures—financial ruin, emotional outbursts, inability to forgive, marital breakup, affairs, and addictions—to the lack of a spiritual dimension in their lives. Whether consciously or subconsciously, people who do not connect with God choose to live their lives without His guidance, intervention, and protection. Sooner or later, there is a high cost to be paid for ignoring the presence and power of God. In our twenties, Roger and I experienced the pain and failure of life without God. Since then, we have spent the rest of our lives trying to stay connected to Him!

FOLLOWING GOD HELPED US FIND EACH OTHER

Our *individual* decisions to follow God led us directly to each other!

From the moment I turned my life over to God, I was compelled to tell anyone who would listen how God had taken away my desire to drink and do drugs, and how He had changed my life so completely. I especially wanted to tell other young people who were searching and struggling that I had found the answer in God! Unsure of how or where to do that, I asked God to show me what to do and where to go. Within the month, the next direction I felt God give me was to move away from my "old" life in California and return home to Cleveland.

Still feeling strongly that I should get involved with high school kids, I drove to my old high school to talk with the principal. He encouraged me to go to the counseling office, where I told a secretary my story. She told me about a youth organization called Campus Life and suggested that I call the club director, Roger Tirabassi, to offer to volunteer for his club. I did!

During the first few months of our friendship, Roger and I talked about everything "under the sun" while working on events, planning meetings, driving to schools, or eating out with all the other staff. During those conversations, we discovered that we had both experienced painful, failed intimate relationships. We talked about those relationships in depth and firmly believed then, as we do now, that the main reason we had failed so miserably was that God was not a part of our lives or our relationships. We were both determined to make God the most important relationship in our lives!

For the first year of our relationship, Roger was my friend, mentor, and club director. Because he suggested that I "use my gift of evangelism in youth ministry," I interned with Campus Life, and by the end of the summer, he was my boss! Soon he became my best friend. Our relationship was built on our mutual love for God, respect for each other, and a desire to help teenagers. In the process, we grew to love and trust each other. One year from the time we met, *though we had never kissed or dated, he asked me to marry him*!

STAYING CONNECTED TO GOD REQUIRES A COMMITMENT OF YOUR TIME

From the beginning of our relationship, Roger challenged me to spend time with God through prayer and Bible reading every day. He would read for a minimum of five minutes a day until he felt God speak to him through a verse, illustration, story, or insight. When we got married in 1978, we decided to grow in our relationship with God *together* and read through the Bible every night, a few chapters at a time. But as the busyness of marriage and ministry wore on, I became haphazard in my approach to growing spiritually.

In 1984, I became acutely aware of my need to stay in touch with God on a daily basis. One Saturday morning in February, at a Youth for Christ conference, I determined to get the spiritual dimension of my life more organized. I made a nonnegotiable decision to spend one hour a day with God—for the rest of my life. Perhaps it was my love for conversation that initially gave me the passion for prayer, but soon the power released through prayer kept me praying! Even more appealing were the intimacy and the accountability that were developing between God and me! After only a few months of one-hour appointments, I developed a prayer notebook, called *My Partner Prayer Notebook*, in which to record my conversations with God.

Roger immediately saw the practicality of the notebook and joined me in journaling, using his own *My Partner Prayer Notebook*! Daily, in the blank journal pages of our separate notebooks, we wrote our prayers and recorded God's answers. Needless to say, five thousand hours later, we have been changed, challenged, corrected, and encouraged to be more nurturing, generous, gentle, quick-to-forgive spouses (and parents)! Staying daily connected to God has absolutely affected *every* aspect of our lives!

The *key* to our success in keeping our daily appointments with God has been that we set aside time with Him one day in advance. As for me, I place my appointment with God on my calendar, scheduling it for the first uninterrupted hour of my day. As for Roger, finding time alone has been a little tougher. Therefore, early in his search for those quiet moments, he purposed to keep his notebook and *One Year Bible* in the bathroom where he was sure to spend time alone daily anyway! (I don't mean to offend anyone with this disclosure, but it has been the consistent time and place where Roger has determined to set aside alone time with God!) *My Partner Prayer Notebook* has been the practical tool, place, and visual reminder that both of us have used for more than thirteen years to stay connected to God!

I have found that the first four sections (Praise, Admit, Request, and Thanks) of my journal allow me to be honest with God about myself, discussing with Him my shortcomings as well as my dreams!

The fifth section of *My Partner Prayer Notebook*, the Listening section, has been especially important to Roger. He begins each day by writing a letter from God to himself on the blank pages within this section. He always begins with, "Dear Roger, I love you very much." This entry is followed by the encouraging words and verses that Roger believes God wants to convey to him. Because it is a common desire of every child to be affirmed by his or her dad, in the Listening sections of *My Partner Prayer Notebook*, Roger and I write the affirmations that we believe God, our Father, speaks to us.

Our goal in journaling our prayers and reading our Bibles has been to communicate with God on a daily basis. As in all intimate relationships, two-way conversations increase transparency, understanding, and honesty. In staying connected with God through daily conversations, we have received those same benefits.

STAYING CONNECTED TO GOD THROUGH CHURCH ATTENDANCE

We know firsthand that to be a churchgoing family must be a lifestyle decision because it is a huge time commitment. Workloads are often longer than forty hours a week for the main wage earner in a family, days off are far and few between, and by the time a "day of rest" comes along, at least one member of a family is wanting to sleep in or *rest*! But the Bible is clear about making a weekly commitment to stay connected to God: "Let us not give up meeting together, as some are in the habit of doing, but let us encourage one another—and all the more as you see the Day approaching" (Heb. 10:25 NIV). It is one of the Ten

Commandments to "keep the Sabbath," but it should also be a desire of our hearts to be in fellowship with God, to stay connected to Him and other believers.

It is all too common in the United States for the wife to drag the whole family to church, often without the husband and/or dad. I have been fortunate. Roger has always been committed to staying connected to God through church attendance, whether we have worked at a church or just been visitors! As a father and husband, he has been committed to be the role model and example for me and Jake in this area. We have never been in a situation or denomination where there was mandatory or recorded attendance, but for all of our married life, we have attended church almost every Sunday!

There are a number of reasons why we attend church:

- To be challenged to grow spiritually
- To enjoy fellowship with other believers
- To have the opportunity to use our spiritual gifts in a local church body

But it is also a place of accountability where we know that we are part of the "bigger" family of God.

Just this morning, Roger spoke to a man he had been repeatedly encouraging to attend church with his family. His friend had been sharing family struggles with him, but had claimed the family was "too busy" to stay connected to God through weekly church attendance. As he shared with Roger this morning a current, devastating family situation, he added, "I just have to get my family back to church." Roger is afraid that in this case, the man may have learned too late the lesson that there is a high cost of not staying connected to God.

STAYING CONNECTED TO GOD THROUGH SERVICE

Roger and I met, and were attracted to each other, in the very place (Campus Life) where we came as individuals to serve God! That is why we often encourage singles to get involved in youth ministry or another ministry where they can volunteer their time and meet other people with similar passions. Over and over, we have enjoyed watching people "meet and marry" while serving on a volunteer or paid ministry staff together. On occasion, it is an instantaneous eruption of similar hearts, minds, goals, and personalities. And in other cases, it is a development of deep respect and fondness that grow over time. But very often, we have found that singles will find *a mate* with whom to serve God once they have found *a place* to serve Him.

Twenty years later, Roger and I are still a couple serving God together in similar or the same capacities as when we first met! And on occasion, we have enjoyed when our son has served in student ministry capacities as well!

STAYING CONNECTED TO GOD IS A DECISION

We offer this chapter as a decision rather than a skill because we know that it is easy for anyone to lose focus in the relationship with God. But as we have personally experienced, if we don't take practical steps to stay connected to God, we can get overwhelmed and distracted by the cares of our lives, jobs, and family responsibilities.

Roger and I are convinced that our individual decisions to stay connected to God *through the practical exercise of journaling our prayers and reading our Bibles* have been the most positive influences upon our intimacy with each other. In addition, our commitment to attend the same church as a couple has drawn us together in worship and has provided us opportunities to use our spiritual gifts in a local church body. Through these practices, we have modeled to our son that moms *and* dads find it incredibly important to stay connected to God in personal and corporate ways.

As we have grown closer to God, we have also grown closer to each other.

■ *Chapter 11* ■

STAY CONNECTED TO EACH OTHER

I n our first year of marriage, we wrestled with the usual but unwelcome adjustments to married life. Our roles, responsibilities, and freedoms were challenged. Conflicting thoughts and feelings caused us to continually struggle with each other. Regularly, we fell into our ugly patterns of escalating anger (Becky) and withdrawal (Roger). We wanted desperately to create new patterns and avoid so much fighting, but we seemed stuck.

After an episode where we had hurt each other, we decided to pray and ask God to help us resolve our conflicts in a better way the next time they occurred. During Roger's quiet time, he felt that God gave him an idea: We should hold hands, even hug, the next time we felt a conflict of this degree surface. It took only three hours for us to have the opportunity to try this new idea because Roger did something that irritated me! Thus, when Rog approached me to hug in the heat of the situation, I became doubly irritated. Not only was I mad, but I wasn't in the "hug" mood. Rather, I wanted Roger to know that he had hurt me. So, as was my habit, I didn't use a very loving approach, and I proceeded to blast him with my anger. But he persisted, wanting to test the new idea and hug me.

He said, "Let's hug while we talk!" I was not agreeable to that, so I backed away. He came closer, and I continued to backpedal.

He said, "You have to hug me. Remember our plan?"

I said, "I don't feel like hugging you. It's your plan. My plan is to be mad at you."

He said, "No, it's God's plan and you agreed to it. You have to hug me!"

As he chased me down the hall, we broke into laughter. In my rush to get away from him, I tripped and fell on the floor, and he dived on top of me! We laughed even harder and then we hugged. By that time, it was hard for me to be angry with Rog. For a while, I forgot what he had done to hurt me so badly and make me so mad. Once I remembered what it was, we took the time to talk it out. In this way Roger and I stayed connected to each other during a heated situation. We encourage you to give this simple method a try in your marriage.

DECIDE TO STAY CONNECTED TO YOUR MATE

Right after we got married—in fact, on our honeymoon—we had a huge argument. Roger felt that I needed to spend more time with him. I thought that I should have the same amount of freedom and independence that I had when I was single. Obviously, our opposing ideas created a problem! It took only three days of marriage for us to realize that we would really have to work through this and many more disagreements to come. We became acutely aware that we had to fight *for* our marriage and use every trick in the book to stay connected to each other.

Through trial and error, and deep commitment to each other, we made three fundamental decisions that helped our relationship grow more secure and intimate. We decided that to stay close to each other we had to do the following:

1. Spend quality *and* quantity time together!
2. *Never* quit!
3. Become each other's best friend and biggest encourager!

SPEND QUALITY AND QUANTITY TIME TOGETHER

Because we met and then married while working in the same organization, we knew something about each other: *Both of us* were inclined to work long, hard hours. Either Roger or I would often stay late and work extra hours to complete a difficult or important project. We were equally susceptible to workaholism if given the right circumstances. The one positive aspect of working in the same organization was that we spent many of our working hours *together*. That was true until I became a mother!

After I gave birth to Jacob, we decided that I would change my employee status from paid staff to volunteer. And very quickly, we saw much less of each other.

We soon realized that we had previously set an unhealthy pattern of working too many hours. (It is not unusual for singles and newlyweds to find themselves in a similar situation.) But now, married and parents, we were being destroyed by that work ethic. I will never forget the day that Roger came home from work after seeing the frustration growing within me, and he said that if I felt his work ever became more important than our marriage, he would change jobs or make the necessary adjustments to reprioritize our lives. I was comforted by his words; I truly believed that he would do whatever he had to do to preserve our marriage.

In year three of our marriage and ministry I felt overwhelmed with the amount of ministry time that consumed our daily lives, and I brought his promise to the table. True to his word, Roger immediately made personal and professional adjustments with the use of his time. They were monumental to me.

1. He agreed to be home *on time rather than late* for dinner. He also scheduled fewer dinner meetings, but more breakfast or lunch meetings.

2. He delegated the club meeting that took him to the east side of Cleveland once a week to a person who lived on that side of town, eliminating a four-hour travel and evening meeting commitment from his weekly schedule. The move also gave a new person the opportunity to exercise leadership gifts.

3. In addition, other time commitments and meetings that he changed or condensed modeled a balanced lifestyle to all who worked for him, showing them, by his actions, that his family was most important to him.

Find the Balance

We worked diligently to find the proper balance between family and work during our first twelve years of marriage, regularly evaluating our jobs and lives, until we came to a new juncture when our son, Jake, went into the sixth grade. At that time, Roger worked for a large church. Due to a number of circumstances, his job began to require much more evening and weekend time away from home. We knew that Jake's entering junior high school would entail a whole new set of time commitments. During that period, I was being asked to speak out of town more frequently. It was a turning point for our family.

That time, Roger brought up our need for a lifestyle revision. He felt as if we were a family spinning out of control and not feeling or staying connected. We all admitted that we were barely holding on. Roger feared that Jake would get shortchanged by having two parents with hectic schedules, and he also was concerned that he and I might start to live two separate lives.

He did something very unusual, even radical, for a man with a doctorate and two master's degrees! He suggested that he resign from his full-time position and work part-time in order to free me to pursue my call and dreams, but allow us still to have a parent at home after school. For Roger, that meant a significant salary reduction. But the same decision allowed me to say yes to the groups calling me to speak! And Jake had a new at-home parent—Dad!

Consider the Cost

Before we made the transition, Roger had to consider the cost of my occasional absence. My traveling meant that some of his regular duties would include cooking, doing laundry, grocery shopping, helping with home-work, and carpooling! (Mind you, he is an *Italian-raised* man!) It was a touching offer that signaled a departure from the traditional roles of married men and women. But because it was his idea, it gave me a huge vote of his con-fidence that it was now God's timing to fulfill my call as a writer and speaker.

Since then, Roger has worked in two different part-time positions. In 1994, he founded Spiritual Growth Min-istries, and he opened his own pastoral counseling office one mile from our house. (If I might say so myself, he is a most wonderful and gifted pastoral counselor.)

In 1991, I began to speak and write, traveling during the school year, but staying home during the summers and for school vacations during our son's junior high and high school years! The decision to limit my speaking primarily to the school year calendar and to one overnight per trip has allowed our family to spend a great deal of time together. In fact, Roger and I have found that we have stayed *more* con-nected in our current roles than when we maintained more traditional roles. We talk and pray by telephone each night that I am out of town, and when I get home, we always have a date planned to go to a movie or out to dinner alone or with other couples. And because I travel often, we have accrued travel miles that provide a yearly family vacation with other families we have met through my speaking engagements, widening our circle of friends!

If You Paid the Price, You'll Reap the Blessings!

Seven years with this schedule have gone by and Jake is off in college! We feel that the decisions we made at the different seasons and junctures in our lives to protect our family time and dating life from the urgency and lure of workaholism have allowed us to stay connected, maintain a wonderful quality of life, and lead *balanced* lives as well as fulfill our individual ministry calls. The personal, spiritual, and relational benefits have been extraordinary! Not only do we enjoy quality time with each other and Jake, but we are doing the very things we love most and are best skilled to do. Though there has been much discussion about the need for *quality* time in relationship building, we believe that both the *quantity* time and the *quality* time make our relationship exciting, satisfying, secure, and fun!

NEVER QUIT!

I'll never forget some scary words I heard from a young friend the week before her wedding. She said, "Well, if it doesn't work, we'll just get a divorce!"

Unfortunately, too many couples are going to the altar with the thought in the back of their minds that if the relationship doesn't work, they will get divorced. We live in an age and society where the tide is moving to prenuptial agreements, broken contracts, litigation, annulments, and irreconcilable differences. This tide is eroding our values as a country, destroying the family and the sanctity of marriage. People would rather quit than change or fight for their relationship.

It is normal to want to quit when we get discouraged or feel overwhelmed, or when a situation feels hopeless. Every relationship will have experiences that yield discouraging, hopeless feelings. Admittedly, some relationships will have more difficulties than others. Therefore, it is important to acknowledge that marriage is difficult *and* to make decisions that will help us succeed. We believe that making a nonnegotiable decision to never divorce is essential to keeping at bay the temptations that inevitably try to threaten all marriages.

Why is it important to make such a strong decision? Because we live in a society that is uncommitted. We cancel our agreements, return our goods, and get our money back. We have taken the fickleness in all aspects of society and adapted it to marriage. The rate of divorce has tripled since the 1960s, and more than 60 percent of new marriages are failing (Michael McManus, *Marriage Savers*, p. 28).

Decide Not to Use the "D" Word

A strong decision never to divorce will give safety and security to a relationship. It provides the marriage an environment for intimacy and bonding. But you need to take your commitment a step farther. When Roger and I got married more than twenty years ago, we decided to never use the "D" word: *divorce*. (You'll remember this is Rule #13 of effective communication.) We felt that even using *the word* would be damaging to our relationship. We didn't want to open the door, even a crack, to let the thought enter our minds. We have kept our word. Closing the door to the very mention of divorce prevented us from even considering bailing out when difficult adjustments and personal differences surfaced. It forced us to search for ways to change, cope, and grow. When we would otherwise choose to abandon, we choose to stay connected and work through our struggles.

Deciding never to quit or use the "D" word not only helps prevent the dissolving of marriages, but can actually be advantageous to a relationship. In *The Secret of Loving*, Josh McDowell cites research demonstrating that commitment to never quit on each other caused attraction to grow, the perceptions of the other person to change, and the individuals to become more loving toward each other (p. 311).

Roger and I backed up our general decision to never quit with some specific decisions that also helped ensure the success of our marriage. We decided to . . .

- talk when we didn't want to,
- make love when we didn't necessarily feel like it,
- save when we wanted to spend,
- work when we would rather play, and
- go to church when we felt like sleeping in!

They were and are hard decisions! (We still have to make them!) They are seldom easy or fun, but they are *essential* to an effective marriage.

BECOME EACH OTHER'S BEST FRIEND AND BIGGEST ENCOURAGER

Laughing at your partner's dumbest jokes, playing games or sports together, enjoying each other's idiosyncrasies, bragging about your better half, and uplifting your spouse with your smile or hug are encouragements every person needs, yet often in the marriage relationship they get ignored! Fun, humor, affirmation, and encouragement are part of the friendship that a spouse should provide. Committing to a "best friend" relationship with your spouse sets the stage for intimacy. We have found that in addition to the financial, spiritual, and emotional support, marriage provides the perfect best friend for us!

Does That Mean We Can't Have Friends of the Opposite Sex?

Early in our marriage—and I can't exactly remember when—Roger and I discussed the fact that we needed to avoid having friends of the opposite sex with whom we would meet in private. In twenty years, we've had many friends, both singles and couples, with whom we socialize. But rarely have we met with these people in private. We enjoy friends and coworkers of the same and opposite sex, but to protect our relationship physically and emotionally, we decided not to confide in our friends or coworkers who are of the opposite sex regarding our marital relationship. We have taken this approach so that we avoid opening any intimate, emotional doors, setting wrong or inappropriate thoughts in motion, or compromising our relationship in any way.

A number of women have been Roger's secretary, and I have been on traveling speaking teams with men. But if or when either of us felt threatened or concerned, we shared our feelings and discussed additional boundaries that might be helpful to protect us! These types of decisions carry some feelings of resistance, but the benefits surpass the negative feelings.

The Three A's: Affirmation, Affection, and Apology

Because Roger does much premarital counseling as well as marriage counseling, he has come up with a system called the Three A's. As a counselor, Roger asks all of his couples to do the Three A's to help them stay connected on a daily basis. As a husband, he encourages us to do the same!

The Three A's are meant to encourage, lift, and love the other person! They are also a practical tool for catching up, patching up, and living up to one's promises! If the Three A's seem corny, *at times,* they are! (But humor often is good for a marriage!)

The Three A's are *affirmation, affection,* and *apology.* Here's how it works. Sometime during the day one person suggests that they do their Three A's. If it hasn't occurred by bedtime, then when the second person gets into bed, it becomes the final opportunity to do the Three A's.

The beauty of his system is that the entire process can be accomplished in three to five minutes. This relieves a couple from having to find a large quantity of time to achieve daily connection on days when time has not been available. Yet it is also a thread that can keep two lives connected!

The first A is affirmation. One partner begins by sharing some behavior the other person did for which you are thankful, such as, "Thank you for helping me do the dishes tonight." Or you can share a quality that you like about the other person by saying, "Thank you for being so gentle with the girls."

As with all of our tools, there are a few rules about affirmations. (Broken rules during the Three A's draw flags, similar to flags thrown during a football game when penalties transpire.) The first rule is not to use any negatives or discounts when giving affirmations. An example of an affirmation with a discount sounds like this: "I like the way you made dinner for me, but it sure would be nice if we could have that type of meal more often." The "but it sure would be nice if . . ." draws a flag. An affirmation cannot contain a negative discount factor. A flag would also be thrown for a statement such as, "Thank you for taking the time to sit at the table and listen to me when you came home from work, *but* I wish you hadn't left the table so soon to go into the den to read the newspaper." When you add the word *but*, you are certain to be breaking a rule! Keep the affirmation purely encouraging!

Here are some examples of positive affirmations:

- "Thank you for taking the time to sit at the table and talk with me after dinner. I appreciated it very much."

- "Thank you for working so hard and providing for our family. We are so fortunate to have such loving support from you."
- "I love the way you dress."
- "I felt so special when you hugged me in front of your friends. Thank you!"
- "I felt so loved when you brought me flowers. Thank you!"
- "Thank you for being so sensitive to my feelings."
- "I admire your generosity."
- "I respect your intelligence. I think you are a very wise person."

The second A is affection. During this time, the goal is to have a time of intentional affection! It is time to give a hug, some form of physical touch, or even a gift. For married couples, it might move right into a sexual experience, or it might merely be the touch of toes, a hug, or a kiss. Here are some forms of the second A:

- Hugging
- Kissing
- Back rubs
- Loving caresses
- Flowers
- Notes
- Cards
- Gifts
- Verbal affection ("I love you" or "You mean the world to me")

The third A is apology. The Bible tells us not to go to sleep holding on to our anger. During this time, you say that you are sorry for any hurt you may have caused the other person. Be very specific with the words you choose. For instance, it would be appropriate to say, "I'm sorry for hurting you by . . . Will you forgive me?"

You are not trying to get too deep into hurts during this three- to five-minute exercise. There will undoubtedly be other times in a given day or week when you delve into hurts that require the use of the conflict resolution and forgiveness processes. You don't go as deep during the daily time designated for the Three A's because you want to keep the exercise fairly short and positive. If you realize that you're going to need more time to resolve a difficult issue, then you could say something like, "We need to find a time to resolve this. What would be a good time to talk about this tomorrow?" Once again, bigger issues should ideally be resolved at times designated or, whenever possible, right at the moment. The third A is to respond to infractions that were overlooked or that occurred when there was not time to handle them or deal with them.

Begin the apology by stating how you think you hurt the other person. If nothing comes to mind, then ask the other person if you did anything that hurt him or her today. If the other person honestly didn't feel hurt that day, it is appropriate to respond, "I can't think of anything!"

Realistically, people in close relationships who spend significant amounts of time together will say or do things that hurt each other almost every day. In most cases, people don't hurt with intention. *They hurt because they are hurt, irritated, or frustrated.*

Here are a few examples of how to share the third A:

- "I'm sorry for being crabby when I came home from work. Will you forgive me?"
- "I'm sorry for being so short with you about your driving. Will you forgive me?"
- "I'm sorry for not noticing that you were all dressed up to go out. Will you forgive me?"

I'm going to be honest with you. Since Roger and I have been married so many years and we know each other's tendencies and personality traits, *I usually initiate* the Three A's. *And* if he did something to bug me that day, I will often cut right to the chase, name his infraction, and forgive him *before* he even has a chance to apologize! He rolls his eyes, and we usually laugh. This little pattern has a way of making his third A easier for both of us!

The commitment to do the Three A's daily must be mutual. In addition, keeping the time limit to three to five minutes will assure continual success with the system. If you need or want more time for discussion, do so at a later time, always keeping the Three A's as a separate time. We have found many couples, including ourselves, have increased their intimacy—and stayed connected on a daily basis—by sticking to this simple, short process. Some couples do the Three A's seven days a week. Others are committed to the process for three to five days a week.

We'd encourage you to try a few different combinations, evaluate what works best for you, then stick to it!

If you can persuade another couple to do or begin the Three A's system, you can encourage and hold each other accountable to maintaining the process. You might call each other twice a week to remind the other couple to keep the system going. It's easy to stop even good things without encouragement and reminders.

ENCOURAGING YOU

Roger and I have found that just feeling "in love" is not enough to have a successful marriage. We have had to learn that love is gaining knowledge, developing skills, and making decisions like those we have shared with you through the pages of this book.

Most importantly, we have both experienced a love from God that changed our lives. Our prayer is that you would also receive God's patience, forgiveness, sacrifice, and kindness—and model that love in all of your relationships. *This* love will change your life!

CHAPTER QUESTIONS

Chapter 1

1. Do you remember anyone in your family saying, "You can't live with them; you can't live without them"? If so, who said it? What was your reaction? What can you relate to in the statement?

2. What do you feel are the benefits you would get from diligently working on improving your relationship?

3. Which relationship phase do you feel you are currently in: the Infatuation Phase, the Reality Phase, or the Adjustment Phase? What do you think will assist you to successfully deal with each phase?

4. Of the following motivations mentioned in Chapter 1 that could keep you and your spouse committed, which ones apply to you? Explain.

    (1) It is unacceptable for us to fail.

    (2) I am determined not to quit.

    (3) I know that blessings will follow if I don't give up.

    (4) I might experience great pain if I stop trying.

    (5) I might leave a positive legacy if I just press on.

    (6) I might create great pain for my children if I leave now.

    (7) I probably will face this same problem with someone else in the future.

    (8) I am aware that nothing great was ever achieved without sacrifice.

(9) I have the conviction of my own word.

(10) All couples struggle; this is not abnormal.

(11) I do not want to disappoint or let other people down.

(12) My spiritual commitment will help me get through this difficult time.

5. Can you share a struggle you currently experience that you find relates to your past? Explain.

Chapter 2

1. Which personality type are you most like?

    _____Sanguine (fun and energetic)

    _____Choleric (leader and developer)

    _____Melancholic (organized and serious)

    _____Phlegmatic (peacemaker and gentle)

    Which of the above would be your secondary type? What are your partner's types?

2. What are five personality strengths you see in yourself and your partner?

3. What are two practical ways these strengths can be used to develop a better relationship with your partner?

4. What are three personality weaknesses you need to work on in your life? How will these weaknesses hurt your relationship if you don't work on them?

5. What are your top five needs? Have your partner rank his or her top five needs.

    1. Affection

    2. Sexual relations

    3. Conversation

    4. Recreational companionship

5. Financial support

6. Attractiveness of spouse

7. Honesty and openness

8. Domestic support

9. Family commitment

10. Admiration

6. List two ways you could meet each of your partner's top five needs:

    Need 1._____ _____

    Need 2._____ _____

    Need 3._____ _____

    Need 4._____ _____

    Need 5._____ _____

7. How do you feel about making a commitment that you will meet at least two of your partner's needs each day?

    _____ I am ready and willing to make the commitment.

    _____ I feel I need a little more time to decide.

    _____ I am not willing yet.

    _____ Other:_____

Chapter 3

1. Of the Fourteen Rules for Effective Communication, which do you think you will struggle with most often? What do you think you can do to help yourself keep the rules?

2. Since saying, "You broke a rule!" is not allowed, what will you say when your partner breaks a rule?

3. Are there any other rules you would like to add to the list of rules? If so, what are they? Is your partner in agreement?

(Remember both of you need to agree before you institute any new rules.)

4. In general, do you use a "fight" or a "flight" response in your relationship? Are there times when you do the other? Explain.

5. Is it easier for you to "speak the truth" or "hold it in" when communicating? Explain why.

6. Do you feel you are better at talking or listening? Explain.

7. Which step of intentional listening is the easiest for you? Which is the most difficult?

    Step One: Listen with awareness (listen for thoughts and feelings).

    Step Two: Paraphrase what you heard (repeat what the other has said).

    Step Three: Inquire (ask questions).

8. Why do you think it is so hard to practice intentional listening? Describe how you will ask your partner to begin the process.

Chapter 4

1. Describe how your parents handled their anger. How did the way that they handled their anger affect you?

2. How do you behave when you become angry? What effect does your behavior have on those around you?

3. Restraining anger can be very difficult. When do you feel most tempted to lose it? What do you think is one way that you can keep from losing control?

4. Before you become angry, you are hurt. What hurt feelings do you experience that are potentially damaging to your relationships?

5. What is your opinion regarding a time-out? How would you and your partner best use this skill in your relationship?

Chapter 5

1. Why do you believe that it is so difficult to ask for forgiveness?

2. What are some minor infractions that you commit regularly?

3. What are some misdemeanors that you have committed? Have you apologized?

4. What are some of the felonies that you don't want to commit?

5. When it becomes difficult for you to forgive, what principle will assist you most?

   (1) *To forgive someone benefits me.*

   (2) *To forgive doesn't mean you allow the person to continue to hurt you in the same way.*

   (3) *Most people don't intentionally try to hurt you.*

   (4) *God wants us to forgive others.*

   (5) *It won't be long before you will need to be forgiven.*

   (6) *Forgiveness becomes easier when you look for similar behavior in your life.*

   (7) *Forgiveness is not a feeling. It is a decision!*

6. Is there anyone whom you feel you have not forgiven? Share what you can do to forgive him or her.

7. Is there anyone you know who is angry with you? What can you do to reconcile the relationship?

Chapter 6

1. Are there any conflicts that you feel you have neglected to resolve? What do you think you can do to resolve them?

2. Is there any area of conflict that comes up regularly in your current relationship? What can you do to handle this in a better way?

3. Have you ever "let the sun go down on your anger"? How did it feel? What can you do in the future to minimize this behavior?

4. Of the six steps in the conflict resolution process, which step do you feel will be the most difficult for you? Explain.

   Step One: Call on God immediately!

   Step Two: Check the time.

   Step Three: Identify the problem.

   Step Four: Brainstorm possible solutions.

   Step Five: Find a solution that we will try.

   Step Six: Try the solution and evaluate its effectiveness.

5. Think of a situation in which you are currently experiencing a conflict. Use the conflict resolution process in an attempt to resolve it. How did you do?

Chapter 7

1. Share the methods that your parents used to manage their finances. What did they believe about money and its management?

2. What decisions have you made regarding money management? Share with your partner how these decisions affect each of you.

3. Have you developed a budget? Why or why not? If so, explain how it is working.

4. What steps do you think you need to take to further your effectiveness in financial management?

5. Share your views on working and its effect on your family. If you haven't answered the questions on page 101, do so now!

6. In the budget worksheet we presented, are there income or expense changes that you need to make that are unique to your situation? We suggest that you prepare a budget as soon as possible.

Chapter 8

1. What were some of the feelings and attitudes that your family had about sex as you grew up? How did your family deal with this topic?

2. How do you think your parents' views regarding sex currently influence your feelings, attitudes, and actions?

3. If you have never discussed the questions on pages 104–105, discuss them with your spouse now.

4. If you currently, or in the future, experience some difficulty in the sexual area of your relationship, what outside help will you seek?

Chapter 9

1. If you don't have children at this time, how many children would you like to have and when? If you do have children, would you like to have more children? If so, how many and when?

2. If you have children, what do you think their personality types are?

3. What are some of the most important values you want to teach your children?

4. What are your feelings and thoughts regarding modeling as a way to teach your children values? In what area of your life do you think this will be difficult, and why?

5. What do you feel are the strengths that your children will possess as a result of their spiritual development?

6. What do you feel is an area that you will have to adjust or change within yourself to become a better parent? How do you think you can go about changing?

7. What are some family traditions that you would like to begin or continue?

8. Share any areas in which you feel you need additional knowledge about or help in regard to parenting. What resources or action steps are you willing to pursue to get that knowledge or help?

Chapter 10

1. Share any areas in your life where not connecting with God has hurt you.

2. Share a time when connecting with God has helped you.

3. Share ways in which you connect to God daily, weekly, and annually. How have these times helped you?

4. Most people struggle with some aspect of prayer. What areas of prayer cause you the most struggle? What steps can you take to overcome those struggles?

5. What spiritual goals would you like to achieve?

6. Share a time in your life when you felt God showed His love to you.

7. As a couple, what are a few ways that you can connect with God together?

Chapter 11

1. Staying connected to each other becomes difficult when we get busy. What do you think you can do to find quantity time together?

2. What are the barriers you will need to overcome to find the quality time?

3. Quality time is also essential—time away from distractions. What will you need to do to find private, uninterrupted time together?

4. Where are some places you would like to go for a vacation? What will the barriers be to working through these hopes? What can you do for vacations?

5. The decision not to use the *divorce* word protects a marriage. How do you feel about such a decision? If the word is used, what will you do to get help?

6. What do you think it will take to maintain a "best friend" relationship?

7. Can you commit to doing the Three A's—a daily discipline for a healthy relationship? When is the best time of day to do them? Who will be the initiator at first?

BIBLIOGRAPHY

Covey, Stephen R. *The 7 Habits of Highly Effective People*. New York: Simon & Schuster, 1989.

Donovan, Mary Ellen, and William P. Ryan. *Love Blocks*. New York: Viking, 1989.

Gray, John. *Men Are from Mars, Women Are from Venus*. New York: HarperCollins, 1993.

Hardin, Jerry, and Dianne Sloan. *Getting Ready for Marriage*. Nashville, Tenn.: Thomas Nelson, 1992.

Harley, Willard F. *His Needs, Her Needs*. Grand Rapids, Mich.: Revell, 1986.

———. *Love Busters*. Grand Rapids, Mich.: Revell, 1992.

Hendrix, Harville. *Getting the Love You Want*. New York: Harper & Row, 1988.

Jensen, Ronald P., and Gina Page. *Spiritual Growth: A Workbook for Group Study*. Costa Mesa, Calif.: R & G Publishing, 1997.

Ketterman, Dr. Grace. *Verbal Abuse: Healing the Hidden Wound*. Ann Arbor, Mich.: Servant, 1992.

LaHaye, Tim. *The Spirit-Controlled Temperament*. Wheaton, Ill.: Tyndale, 1966.

———. *Your Temperament: Discover Its Potential*. Wheaton, Ill.: Tyndale, 1984.

Littauer, Florence. *Personality Plus!* Grand Rapids, Mich.: Revell, 1992.

Littauer, Florence, and Marita Littauer. *Personality Puzzle*. Grand Rapids, Mich.: Revell, 1992.

McDowell, Josh. *The Secret of Loving*. Wheaton, Ill.: Tyndale, 1985.

McManus, Michael J. *Marriage Savers*. Grand Rapids, Mich.: Zondervan, 1993.

Markman, Howard, Scott Stanley, and Susan L. Blumberg. *Fighting for Your Marriage: Positive Steps for Preventing Divorce and Preserving a Lasting Love*. San Francisco, Calif.: Josey-Bass, 1994.

Nicholson, David. *What You Need to Know Before You Fall in Love*. Nashville, Tenn.: Thomas Nelson, 1995.

Penner, Clifford L., and Joyce J. Penner. *52 Ways to Have Fun, Fantastic Sex*. Nashville, Tenn.: Thomas Nelson, 1994.

————. *Getting Your Sex Life off to a Great Start*. Dallas, Tex.: Word, 1994.

————. *Restoring the Pleasure*. Dallas, Tex.: Word, 1993.

Rosenau, Douglas. *A Celebration of Sex*. Nashville, Tenn.: Thomas Nelson, 1994.

————. *Slaying the Marriage Dragon*. Wheaton, Ill.: Victor, 1991.

Schmidt, Teresa. *Anger Management and Violence Prevention*. Minneapolis: Johnson Institute, 1993.

Stoop, David, and Stephen Arterburn. *The Angry Man*. Dallas: Tex.: Word, 1991.

Virkler, Henry A. *Broken Promises: Healing and Preventing Affairs in Christian Marriages*. Dallas, Tex.: Word, 1992.

INDEX OF THE KNOWLEDGE, SKILLS, AND DECISIONS NECESSARY FOR SUCCESSFUL RELATIONSHIPS

Three Phases of Every Relationship   8–10
Twelve Motivators to Succeed in a Relationship   17
Three Truths About Relationships   19
Personality Inventory   25–27
Fourteen Rules for Effective Communication   50
Three Steps of Intentional Listening   56–61
Six Quick Steps to Control Your Anger   72
Three Levels Requiring Forgiveness   75–77
Seven Motivators for Extending Forgiveness   80–83
Six-Step Conflict Resolution System   92–94
Sample Budget   98–99
List of Questions Regarding Sex   104–5
Ten Positive Parenting Skills   113–33
The Three A's—Affirmation, Affection, and
    Apology   158–63

ABOUT THE AUTHORS

Becky Tirabassi is a renowned motivational speaker and bestselling author of *Change Your Life, Let Prayer Change Your Life, Let Faith Change Your Life,* and numerous other books. As a guest contributor on *The CBS Early Show* in 2001, Becky appears regularly on television and radio, inspiring audiences across the country to change their lives for the better. She has appeared on *Fox and Friends, Focus on the Family,* and several other national programs. She is the president and founder of Becky Tirabassi Change Your Life®, Inc., a multi-media company. She also maintains an extensive national speaking tour.

Roger Tirabassi, M.A., M.S., D. Min, is a pastoral counselor and founder of Spiritual Growth Ministries, a non-profit organization that focuses on premarital and marital counseling and couples seminars. He has earned a Doctorate of Ministry degree and Masters Degree in Pastoral Counseling and is a member of the American Association for Psychological Studies.

Together, Roger and Becky Tirabassi yearly host Let Love Change Your Life seminars for couples across America. The Tirabassis have been married for 24 years and are the proud parents of one son, Jacob. They currently live in Newport Beach, California.

Becky Tirabassi
Change Your Life, Inc.
P.O. Box 9672
Newport Beach, CA 92660

phone: (800) 444-6189
fax: (949) 644-8044
website: www.changeyourlifedaily.com

ALSO BY BECKY TIRABASSI

Let Faith Change Your Life

A look at how real faith can revolutionize your life. You'll be encouraged to open your heart to the life-changing force of faith.

0-7852-7235-6
Hardcover
192 pages

Let Prayer Change Your Life

A tool for transforming your prayer life. You'll discover the awesome power of, empowering discipline of, and ultimate design for prayer.

0-7852-6885-5
Softcover
144 pages

Workbook
0-7852-7746-3

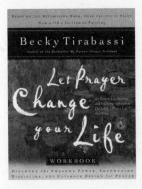

My Prayer Partner Notebook

This detailed prayer organizer offers an easy-to-use system for developing a disciplined prayer life.

0-7852-7490-0
Softcover
276 pages